PRAISE FOR
The Trolley Problem

"Does the sacredness of our fundamental right to life trump the utility of doing the greatest good for the greatest number? If harming an innocent person was not the intention but was a foreseeable consequence of our action—as in drone strikes—how are we to judge this? Cathcart's new book brings out the inner moral philosopher hidden in all of us: It gets us to think about the importance of moral reasoning by luring us into doing it."

—KENNETH SHARPE,
coauthor of *Practical Wisdom:
The Right Way to Do the Right Thing*

"Clearly written and dramatically presented, Thomas Cathcart's *The Trolley Problem* is an excellent introduction to ethics. It's a pedagogical classic."

—JOHN PERRY,
Emeritus Professor of Philosophy, Stanford University,
and author of *The Art of Procrastination*

"Entertaining, informative, and presented in an original format. I would recommend it to anyone looking for a sympathetic route through the big moral questions of the day."

—ROBERT ROWLAND SMITH,
author of *Breakfast with Socrates*

"Stop! Before you throw anyone off the bridge or under the bus, grab this witty, intelligent, and fast-paced treatise on ethical reasoning and chuckle your way to fresh moral insight. With Tom Cathcart as your guide, you'll discover the pleasure of ethics without the sermon."

—MARVIN M. ELLISON,
ethicist and author of *Making Love Just*

"Cathcart's probing exploration of the complex nuances of moral reasoning takes you on an intellectual journey both stimulating and educational. This riveting little book is grounded, relevant, and fun. If you enjoy wrestling with ethical challenges, it's a must read."

—GREGORY STOCK,
author, *The Book of Questions*

"Clang, clang, clang goes the trolley problem! Join Tom Cathcart on a wild ride through the various permutations of this philosophical puzzle, as he picks up such disparate passengers as Jeremy Bentham, Immanuel Kant, Thomas Aquinas, Friedrich Nietzsche, and Peter Singer along the way. While there may be blood on the tracks, Cathcart will guide you to a thought-provoking final stop."

—TIM MADIGAN,
Associate Professor of Philosophy,
St. John Fisher College and columnist,
Philosophy Now magazine

THE TROLLEY PROBLEM

——— *Or* ———

Would You Throw the Fat Guy Off the Bridge?

THE TROLLEY PROBLEM

—— *Or* ——

Would You Throw the Fat Guy Off the Bridge?

A PHILOSOPHICAL CONUNDRUM

THOMAS CATHCART

WORKMAN PUBLISHING
NEW YORK

Library of Congress Cataloging-in-Publication Data is available.

ISBN 978-0-7611-7513-1

Design by Sarah Smith

Jacket/casewrap illustration by Serge Seidlitz

Photo Credits: p.17 Georgios Kollidas/fotolia; p.25 nickolae/fotolia;
p.32 Universal History Archive/Getty Images; p.48 Georgios Kollidas/
fotolia; p.61 Pictorial Press Ltd/Alamy Images; p.80 Steve Pyke/Getty
Images; p.84 nickolae/fotolia; p.113 Interfoto/Alamy Images

Workman books are available at special discounts when purchased in
bulk for premiums and sales promotions as well as for fund-raising or
educational use. Special editions or book excerpts can also be created
to specification. For details, contact the Special Sales Director at the
address below, or send an email to specialmarkets@workman.com.

Workman Publishing Company, Inc.
225 Varick Street
New York, NY 10014-4381
workman.com

WORKMAN is a registered trademark of
Workman Publishing Co., Inc.

Printed in the United States of America
First printing August 2013

10 9 8 7 6 5 4 3 2 1

ACKNOWLEDGMENTS

////////////////////////////

A number of smart and generous people reviewed earlier drafts of the book and provided some very creative suggestions. Thanks to my friend Dr. Peter King for his careful analysis of the trolley problem and his provision of several real-world examples. Thanks also to the other members of the King family for their participation in the discussions around the dining room table.

My oldest and dearest friend, Danny Klein, offered loads of encouragement and several great ideas, and his voice was constantly in my head, telling me to make it clearer, slow down, take more steps. As my mentor on a number of books we wrote together, Danny literally taught me how to write a book. Thank you, Danny.

I am fortunate to have two extraordinarily strong women in my life. My wife, Eloise, an excellent writer and editor, read several drafts and improved each of them considerably, but her never-flagging encouragement, support, and love were even more important to me. Thank you, Eloise.

My daughter, Esther, is a much-loved chaplain to many people and dogs, and I am very lucky to be among the beneficiaries of her funny, loving spirit.

Margot Herrera, my editor at Workman, cheerfully ignored my defensiveness and kept urging me to improve the manuscript. Thank you, Margot. Your ideas were excellent.

And a big thank-you to my agent, Julia Lord, who shares an attribute with God: Without her there would be nothing.

CONTENTS

////////////////////////////

THE TROLLEY PROBLEM

PROBLEM

Or

Would You Throw the Fat Guy Off the Bridge?

PROLOGUE

////////////////////////////

The Problematic Trolley

A thought experiment first published in a technical philosophy journal in Britain nearly fifty years ago has unexpectedly become a popular brainteaser on college campuses, and in faculty lounges, family dining rooms, general interest magazines, and academic journals around the world. Dubbed "the trolley problem," it has given birth to a mini-industry, jokingly referred to as "trolleyology." Trolleyologists these days include philosophers, psychologists, neuroscientists, evolutionary theorists, and ordinary laypeople.

The original trolley problem, created by British philosopher Philippa Foot in 1967, was short and simple: A driver of a runaway tram sees five people ahead on the track. He can either allow the tram to stay on the main track, thereby killing them all—for an unstated reason, they are unable to get off the track—or he can steer the tram onto a sidetrack, where only one person will be hit and killed. Should he steer the tram onto the less-occupied track, killing one person rather than five? Furthermore, she wondered, how does this scenario differ from, say, one in which doctors could save the lives of several people by killing one person and making a serum from his dead body? Most of us, Foot thought, would approve of steering the tram onto the sidetrack to minimize the number of casualties and would disapprove of killing the man to obtain the serum. And she found the question of the difference between the two scenarios intriguing.

In 1985, an American philosopher named Judith Jarvis Thomson expanded the scenario a bit: This time *you* see the trolley barreling down the track out of control, and you are standing by a switch. You can do nothing and allow it to hit and kill the five, or you can throw the switch and detour the trolley so that it hits and kills only the one person on the siding. The principal new element is that, unlike the trolley driver, you have no professional responsibility to choose between the two tracks. You can, if you choose, do nothing. It could be said, of course, that the trolley driver could also do nothing and stay on the main track, but his job involves making constant decisions about which track to take, so his "doing nothing" is, at the very least, more ethically complex than that of the innocent bystander. Thomson's less freighted version of the problem is: Should you, the bystander, do nothing and let fate take its course, or should you pull the switch, causing one person to die but saving five?

Both philosophers contrasted their scenarios with others that appeared similar in many ways but were arguably different in other ways. The best known is Thomson's scenario in which you are standing on a footbridge over the trolley track. There is no switch; there is no siding. There is only a single track with five people on it beyond the footbridge, and they will all be killed if you do nothing. You realize that the only action that can save the five people is for you to drop a heavy weight in front of the trolley to stop it. The only object nearby that is heavy enough to stop the trolley is a very fat man standing next to you on the footbridge. Should you push him off the bridge in order to save the five? And is that—or is it not—essentially the same thing as throwing the switch?

Since then, philosophers, psychologists, and brain scientists have been trying to explain why most of us feel justified in pulling the switch but not in throwing the man. More and more trolley scenarios have appeared, as trolleyologists have tried to pinpoint exactly what it is that seems different about throwing the switch versus throwing the man. Or . . . are they in fact really different at all? Princeton University philosophy professor Kwame Appiah has said that the huge and growing body of hair-splitting commentary "makes the Talmud look like CliffsNotes."

Philosophers, psychologists, and brain scientists have been trying to explain why most of us feel justified in pulling the switch but not in throwing the man.

Some philosophers—and many more casual observers—have wondered out loud about the value of such thought experiments. Real-life decisions are, after all, considerably richer and more complex, as well as less farfetched, than the question of whether to throw a switch to divert a runaway trolley.

Others have argued, however, that such thought experiments, by their very simplicity, can help us clarify the way we make—or should make—more complicated ethical decisions. Philippa Foot's 1967 article, for example, was intended to shed light on some of the ethical questions raised by the issue of abortion, such as whether it is morally permissible for Catholics to undergo a hysterectomy to save the life of the mother, even though it will have what they believe to be a bad consequence, the termination of a pregnancy. Finally, while reading most academic philosophy is often tough slogging for those of us who are not professional philosophers, the trolley problem is, happily, accessible.

Over the years, scholars in other academic disciplines have become intrigued by the trolley problem. In 2003, a team of Harvard University psychologists created a website called the Moral Sense Test, in which visitors were invited to record their reactions to various trolley scenarios. For their initial study, the researchers wanted 5,000 participants; within weeks, they had met their goal. More than ten years later, the website is still active and still drawing visitors in huge numbers.

In 2009, Harvard University took its first full step into online learning when it made professor of government Michael Sandel's popular undergraduate course on justice available for credit on the Internet and for more casual viewing on PBS. Professor Sandel led off the first lecture with the trolley problem, and the reaction was viral. Because the lecture is available online through several points of entry, it is difficult to know exactly how many people have viewed it, but the YouTube version of the PBS video alone has had 4.4 million hits, three times the number of online viewers who watched LeBron James's 2010 decision to "take his talents to South Beach."

The trolley problem has raised questions upon questions and questions within questions—just as philosophers since Socrates have always done—and it has inspired late-night bull sessions around the world. But up until very recently, the trolley problem has seemed to most people to be a clever, philosophical puzzle: fascinating, intriguing, a little whimsical.

Then the event happened.

THE NEWSPAPER STORY

////////////////////////

Trolley "Heroine" Charged with Manslaughter
D.A. Calls Recipient of City's Valor Award "Outlaw," Cites "Dangerous Precedent"

THE GAZETTE
Tuesday, January 22, 2013

(San Francisco) District Attorney Cleveland Cunningham yesterday announced the grand jury indictment of Daphne Jones of Oakland in the trolley death of Chester "Chet" Farley of San Francisco last October. Ms. Jones was honored by the mayor in December for "showing extraordinary quick-wittedness and valor," when she threw a switch and diverted a runaway trolley onto a siding. The trolley would surely have hit and killed five people if it had continued on the main track, but instead it killed only Mr. Farley, who was standing on the siding. Mr. Cunningham stated that the grand jury had correctly come to the conclusion that Ms. Jones "had no right to play God" when she decided that it was better for Mr. Farley to die than the five others.

Mr. Farley's daughter, Sondra Farley, was present at the news conference and said that she is hopeful that the future conviction of Ms. Jones will help the family "reach closure." The *Gazette* has learned that the family also has a civil suit pending against both San Francisco Muni and Ms. Jones.

Reached for comment, Sally Jo Kariakidis, one of the five whose lives were spared when Ms. Jones threw the switch, said, "I am so grateful that Ms. Jones was there and was able to think so quickly. I certainly sympathize with Mr. Farley's family, but I don't think that Ms. Jones should be blamed for doing what most of us would have done to minimize the number of casualties from the accident. I hope that doesn't sound heartless, particularly since I am one of the five who survived." Ms. Kariakidis has appeared with Ms. Jones at several public events, most recently a December fund-raiser for the Bay Area Straphangers Association, a trolley safety advocacy organization.

Bay Area residents attending the news conference appeared split in their reaction to the news of Ms. Jones's indictment. A smattering of applause was heard when Mr. Cunningham announced the grand jury's decision. But Floyd Carlucci of Sausalito told reporters that he thought Ms. Jones had made the right choice in pulling the switch. "Do the math," he said.

District Attorney Cunningham said that he realized that the decision of the grand jury "would probably not be popular in all quarters," and he commended them for taking a difficult stand. "It would be a dangerous precedent indeed if we allowed one person to make life-or-death decisions that favor some of our citizens over others," he said.

The *Gazette* has obtained the original police report of the incident. It can be seen on our website, gazette.com.

THE POLICEMAN'S STATEMENT

////////////////////////////

Incident Report

Filed by Patrolman LeRoy Takahashi

SAN FRANCISCO POLICE DEPARTMENT
Friday, October 5, 2012

At approximately 4:49 p.m. on October 5, 2012, Patrolwoman Sarah Foster and I received a call from our dispatcher, advising us to proceed to the corner of California Street and Van Ness Avenue, where a trolley had apparently run over a man, causing "grievous injury or death." Patrolwoman Foster and I proceeded to the aforesaid corner, where we observed a city ambulance crew placing the body of a Caucasian male, approximately fifty years of age, into an emergency vehicle. A trolley was parked on the siding, just beyond the site of the alleged accident.

A woman approached us in an agitated state and

identified herself as Daphne Jones, 3 Clark Street, Oakland, age twenty-seven. She reported that she had thrown a trolley switch beside the track and diverted the trolley onto the siding where the alleged accident had occurred. We inquired as to why she had acted in this manner, and she indicated that it was in order to save the lives of five other persons who were standing on the main track. We instructed her to remain in our vehicle while we conducted a surveillance of the area and interviewed witnesses.

After speaking with several eyewitnesses, we determined that Ms. Jones's account of the incident was accurate. Upon checking with SFPD HQ, we were informed that no apparent crime had occurred, as Ms. Jones's conduct appeared to meet Exception 3 to Section 192, Manslaughter: "Killing another person when you kill to protect yourself *or another* from being killed or suffering great bodily injury does not constitute manslaughter, either voluntary or involuntary." We advised Ms. Jones that she might be contacted again by the district attorney's office, but that for now she was free to go. She was still quite agitated, so we drove her to her home and notified our dispatcher at approximately 7:15 p.m.

THE JURY OFFICER'S CIVICS LESSON

///////////////////////

Jurors' Welcome

Commissioner of Jurors' Office

COURT OF PUBLIC OPINION
Monday, April 1, 2013

Good morning, prospective jurors. I'm Margaret Sturdevant-Casey, chief jury officer here in the Court of Public Opinion, and it is my pleasure to welcome you here this morning. I hope everyone has found the coffee machine here to my right and the restrooms just beyond the glass doors.

This morning we'll begin jury selection in the case of *The People v. Daphne Jones.* Twelve of you will be chosen to sit in the jury box and serve as the jurors of record, but, unlike cases in other courts, *all* of you will serve as associate jurors, because here in the Court of Public

Opinion, everyone's opinion matters. This means that, barring serious illness, you must follow the case on television or online and submit your input to the jury when it begins its deliberations. This is, after all, the Court of *Public* Opinion, and it is only for obvious practical reasons that we must choose twelve to represent all of you in the deliberations. Those of you who aren't seated still have a responsibility to inform yourselves of the facts and arguments in this case and, if possible, form an opinion.

In addition to this requirement of universal participation, the Court of Public Opinion also enjoys a unique status above and beyond that of any other court in the nation. You probably learned in your high school civics course, as I did in mine, that the Supreme Court is the highest court in the land. Well, I'm here to tell you this morning that this is not strictly true. The Court of Public Opinion is actually the highest court in the land. How so? First, while the Supreme Court can strike down a law that is presently on the books by finding that it is incompatible with the U.S. Constitution, the Supreme Court is absolutely unable to create a new law. By contrast, the Court of Public Opinion can and does inspire the creation of new laws nearly every day. That is to say, the laws passed by our representatives in Congress generally reflect a broad public consensus, albeit imperfectly. Second, while the Supreme Court has the sole authority to *interpret* the Constitution, only the Court of Public Opinion can *change* the Constitution, as it in fact has done twenty-seven times over the course of the past two hundred twenty–plus years.

If there were no Court of Public Opinion with the authority to change the Constitution, women would not be able to vote today. Laws permitting one person to own another person would in all probability still be in force. And laws governing private behavior in the bedrooms of consenting adults would likely still exist in some states. So I think you can see that your responsibility as jurors on this court—or, if you prefer, citizens in this democracy—is literally awesome.

So, with that, I welcome you to the duty and privilege that come with being a juror in the Court of Public Opinion.

THE PROSECUTOR'S THRUST

////////////////////////

Summation by District Attorney Cleveland Cunningham

COURT OF PUBLIC OPINION
Friday, April 19, 2013

Ladies and gentlemen of the jury, after three weeks of testimony, you have now heard all the evidence in this matter. It is now time for me to summarize the people's case against the defendant, Daphne Jones.

You all know the facts. The defendant was walking down the street when she saw a trolley coming down the track at a high rate of speed, obviously unable to stop. She noticed a switch nearby and deliberately threw that switch, sending the trolley down a siding and into a man, who she knew or should have known would be hit and killed by the trolley. We submit that Ms. Jones is therefore guilty of voluntary manslaughter.

Now, the defense team, led by Ms. Baumgarten, would have us believe that mitigating facts in this situation prevent it from rising to the level of manslaughter—or, in fact, any criminal charge. Indeed, they contend that Ms. Jones should be acclaimed as a heroine, because, in killing this one man, she saved the lives of five other people. They cite the nineteenth-century British ethicist Jeremy Bentham, who wrote that the rightness or wrongness of an act depends entirely upon its consequences and that our actions should be guided by the principle of creating the greatest happiness for the greatest number of people. This philosophy has been given various labels, including consequentialism, for obvious reasons. It has also been called utilitarianism, meaning that "good" simply means "whatever is most useful in maximizing happiness." We will deal at length here today with the inadequacy of this philosophy as a basis for either legal or ethical decision-making.

The prosecution does not quarrel with the defense's representation of the facts. We concede that there were, in fact, five other people on the main track. We even concede that the defendant drew the correct conclusion that

JEREMY BENTHAM (1748–1832)

Soon after Bentham was born in London, it became clear to his family that he was a child prodigy. He read a lengthy history of England while still a toddler and began his study of Latin when he was three. At the age of twelve, he entered Queen's College. Upon graduating, he studied law and was admitted to the bar but never practiced. Philosopher that he was, he preferred to dedicate his life to writing about how to reform the British legal system along utilitarian lines: the greatest happiness for the greatest number.

While others were arguing from "natural law" as the basis for maintaining privilege, Bentham took radical social stands on the basis of "utility," or the maximization of happiness in society. He strongly influenced the elimination of debtor prisons in England, the reform of parliamentary representation, and the establishment of a civil service sector accessible to all classes by way of an examination. In opposition to the "natural law" theorists, he also advocated universal suffrage and the decriminalization of homosexuality.

those five people would have died if she had allowed the trolley to proceed on the main track. We further concede that from a utilitarian or consequentialist perspective, Ms. Jones's behavior was "ethical," even praiseworthy, because it led to the death of only one man.

As you know, no criminal charges have been brought against Ms. Jones in municipal or state court, presumably because no prosecutor in the lower jurisdictions believed he or she could win this case before a jury. The prosecuting attorneys who pondered whether to proceed with this case may themselves have felt that the circumstances are exculpatory. Or they may have wished to bring the case forward but knew that a jury would be swayed by their emotions and sympathize with the defendant, or perhaps with the five who were spared. For whatever reason, charges have not been brought. And that, ladies and gentlemen, is why the case is being brought here—to the Court of Public Opinion.

The court officer has already instructed you in the unique mission of this court. Let me add that we on the prosecution team are fully aware of the burden of proof that is ours in this case. By this I do not mean the burden that the prosecution normally has: that a defendant is innocent unless and until proven guilty beyond a reasonable doubt. That burden applies to prosecutors and juries in lower jurisdictions: municipal, state, and federal criminal courts. The prosecution in the Court of Public Opinion does not carry that burden. We are free to argue in any way we choose, and you are free to decide in any way you choose.

Most jurors in this court would probably stipulate that they are nonetheless bound by a few *ethical* requirements: for example, that the facts, while we cannot help but interpret them, should not be deliberately altered or disregarded and that we should be led by a chain of reasoning rather than by unbridled emotion or bias. Emotion and bias are probably unavoidable—and emotion may even play a positive role in decision-making—but most jurors seem to agree that conclusions based on emotion and bias must at the very least be consistent with an appeal to reason. In other words, their conclusions must be reasonable.

No, the burden that the prosecution bears in this case is not proof beyond a reasonable doubt, and the ethical demands—that we stick to the facts (as we see them) and that we be reasonable—are a light burden for both prosecutors and jurors. The special burden for the prosecution in this particular case is that "common sense" would seem to be on the side of the defense. Indeed, this is probably the main reason that this case has not been brought in a lower court. My job today will be to convince you that "common sense" in this case is simply nonsense.

Before it was possible to circumnavigate the globe, it was "common sense" that the world was flat.

First, a word about common sense. Before it was possible to circumnavigate the globe, it was "common sense" that the world was flat. Before the careful observations and complex mathematics of Copernicus, it was "common sense" that the sun moved around the Earth. Before the discovery of the fossil record, it was "common sense" that the world was only a few thousand years old.

Until quite recently, it was "common sense" that men should be given more authority in our society than women. Right now, the "commonsense" view that marriage is between one man and one woman is being supplanted in several states by a very different view.

So, while we, the prosecution, are not naïve about the fact that we bear a heavy burden in arguing against common sense, we are challenged by the great discoveries of the past to prove "common sense" wrong once again.

Our argument this morning will be based on a compelling precedent, a prior case in which a huge majority of the Court of Public Opinion found the defendant guilty of a strikingly similar crime. First, we will lay out for you the facts of this precedent case. Then we will argue that the precedent case is, in all important ways, quite similar to the case before you. It is here that we will mount our attack against "common sense," because the defense will try to convince you that it is "common sense" that there are important differences between the two cases that dictate that you arrive at very different verdicts. I am confident that you will not be bamboozled by this misleading argument and will find Daphne Jones guilty as charged.

The precedent case is that of Dr. Rodney Mapes, a trauma surgeon called to the emergency room in a large teaching hospital in Philadelphia. A terrible multicar collision had just occurred on a nearby interstate highway, and six patients had been rushed to Dr. Mapes's hospital. Triaging the six, Dr. Mapes quickly determined that two patients needed kidney transplants; the third needed a heart transplant; the fourth, a liver transplant; and the fifth, a lung transplant. Mapes was worrying about where he could possibly find donors for these patients when he discovered that the sixth patient, a thirty-five-year-old male, had been sent to the hospital for observation and had no apparent injuries at all. Mapes then had the young man sent to the operating room, removed all of his organs, and transplanted them into the other five patients, thereby saving their lives. At his trial, Dr. Mapes memorably said, "Well, I figured it was better that one patient should die rather than five die." Ladies and gentlemen of the jury, you will remember that these are almost the identical words that you heard Ms. Jones use to defend her pulling of the switch. They are the words of utilitarians and consequentialists! And, in the Court of Public Opinion, they were found to be diabolical words—yes, words of the devil! The jury of your peers found Dr. Mapes guilty of murder in the first degree.

Interviews with the jurors after the trial uncovered the reasoning that went into their decision. Several jurors asked some variation of the question "Who is Dr. Mapes to play God? What gives him the right to decide who lives and who dies?" Yes, while they recognized that on the surface it might appear that it is better for one to die than for five, they insisted that there is much more to making an ethical decision than calculating what has the happiest consequences for the greatest number. At some point, they said, we have to consider questions of rights. One juror, a professor of philosophy at the University of California, Berkeley, cited the eighteenth-century German philosopher, Immanuel Kant. According to Kant, the professor said, it is always wrong to treat people merely as means rather than as ends in themselves. The sixth man had been *used*—solely as a means of saving the others, with no consideration for his *right* to not have his personhood violated and, indeed, his very life taken.

Dr. Mapes considered the sacrificed man only a number—patient #6, to be exact—and compared him with the greater number of the group saved. But patient #6 was a human being. He had a name: Bob Titherington. He had a life: He was a house painter with a wife and three young kids. He liked to play golf, and he coached his son's Little

League team. He had a *right* not to be deliberately sacrificed. This Kantian view has been called *deontological*, from the Greek *deon*, meaning duty. From a deontological standpoint, morality consists of carrying out *duties* toward those who have various *rights*, and not of simply calculating the course of action with the most utility for the most people.

In contrast to Bob Titherington's right not to have his life taken from him, the professor argued, the five patients who were saved had no particular right to be saved. We can assume that they would have *desired* to be saved, that they were perhaps *grateful* to be saved (particularly if they weren't told at what price their lives had been bought), but they had no inherent *right* to be saved.

So what about the case before you? Did not the man on the siding have a *right* not to be deliberately run over by a trolley? The five who were saved had no particular right to be saved from a runaway trolley, but the man on the siding did have a right to not be deliberately killed by a trolley guided by Ms. Jones. In short, who gave Ms. Jones the right to play God?

The professor pointed out that Kant also said that we should act only according to a rule that we would want to

IMMANUEL KANT (1724–1804)

Kant was born and raised and spent his entire adult life in and around the Prussian city of Königsberg. He never married, and the high point of his day, aside from philosophizing, was his walk—which he always took at precisely the same time. Rumor had it that the keeper of the town clock actually set it according to Kant's stroll.

His rootedness and austerity cast some light on the sort of philosopher Kant was: He used his reason to reflect on . . . the limits of reason. His best-known book, *Critique of Pure Reason*, explores the limits of what our minds can know about the world outside our minds. His so-called second critique, *Critique of Practical Reason*, delves into the limits of what we can know about how we ought to act. The two maxims cited in the trial of Dr. Mapes—that we should treat other human beings as ends in themselves and that we should act only according to rules that we would want to become universal laws—both stem from Kant's exploration of the nature and boundaries of moral reason itself. (If that connection isn't clear to you, don't worry! It took Kant many pages of dense prose to explain it, an exercise that we will not repeat here.) Suffice it to say that Kant's sole interest was in reason looking at itself. No wonder he was content to sit, think, write, and walk.

become a universal law. Ladies and gentlemen, would you want to live in a society in which the state could enter this courtroom here today, seize you, and harvest both your kidneys, because there was greater utility in saving two people whose kidneys were failing? Utilitarianism is an inadequate response to ethical dilemmas—and if it were a universal law, we would approve not only the actions of Ms. Jones, but also those of Dr. Mapes and a hypothetical band of state-sponsored enforcers of the greatest happiness for the greatest number, like our imagined kidney police!

We just tried to imagine a universal law that demands that we always seek the greatest happiness for the greatest number. In this country, we have an *actual* universal law that is designed precisely to *prevent* a consistent utilitarianism: the U.S. Constitution. The founders of our nation created the Constitution to preclude what they called the tyranny of the majority. They had the wisdom to see that unbridled utilitarianism could lead to the majority's simply stripping the minority of their lives, their liberty, or their property if, by doing so, they created more good for more people. In effect, they foresaw the real possibility of the kidney police. What they recognized is that we human beings have some universal *rights* that other people may not override in the name of utility.

Therefore, in conclusion, ladies and gentlemen, do not be fooled by the specious, utilitarian arguments of Ms. Baumgarten and her defense

Utilitarianism is an inadequate response to ethical dilemmas.

team. Put aside "common sense" and acknowledge that "common sense" in this case creates a very dangerous precedent. And put aside any emotional bond you may feel with Ms. Jones because you think that in similar circumstances you might well have chosen to act as she did. I daresay that we might all have acted as Ms. Jones did. But think of the man on the siding and his rights. Remember that he, too, had a name, Chet Farley. Remember that he loved to play the piano at the local VFW and that he was the perennial Santa Claus at their Christmas party. And remember that his personhood was violated by a deliberate act perpetrated by Ms. Jones. If you remember Mr. Farley's rights, I am confident that you will find Ms. Jones guilty of manslaughter.

THE DEFENSE ATTORNEY'S PARRY

////////////////////////////

Closing Statement by Defense Attorney
Martha Baumgarten

THE COURT OF PUBLIC OPINION
Friday, April 19, 2013

Oh, my! Where to begin? The prosecution has made a case so bizarre that I must pause a moment to think how to respond. Contrary to common sense? Contrary to any sense, I'd say!

District Attorney Cunningham cites a so-called precedent that varies so dramatically from the case before you that to call it a "precedent" insults one's intelligence. But of that, more later.

First, I ask you to consider a case that is nearly *identical* to the case of Ms. Jones, a case that was heard in this very court, the Court of Public Opinion. And, interestingly enough, another case, one that is nearly identical to the case of Dr. Mapes, has also been heard in this court *by the very same jury.* Very different verdicts were handed down by that jury in the two cases.

A team of psychologists at Harvard University brought both these cases to the Court of Public Opinion in 2003. A jury of some 5,000 members was seated and heard the evidence in the two cases online.

In the first case, a woman named Clara Murphy was a passenger on a trolley whose driver had fainted. Clara faced the very same dilemma as Daphne Jones. She could allow the trolley to continue on the main track, killing five people standing on the track, or she could steer the trolley onto a siding, killing one man. A resounding 89 percent of the jury thought that it was morally permissible for Clara to steer the trolley onto the siding.

The same jury heard the case of Frank Tremaine. Frank was standing on a footbridge over a trolley track, when an out-of-control trolley came hurtling down the track headed for five people standing on the track beyond the footbridge. There was no siding on which to deflect the trolley. Frank quickly determined that the only way to stop the trolley was to drop a heavy weight onto the track.

Unfortunately, there were no large objects on the bridge, but there was a portly man standing next to Frank. Frank saw that he could either shove the man off the footbridge and into the path of the trolley, killing the man but saving the five, or he could allow the five to be killed. He chose to push the man. Ladies and gentlemen, only a meager 11 percent of the jury thought that Frank was justified in shoving that man into the path of the trolley.

The prosecution would no doubt want us to believe that these two cases are so similar that the jury should have brought the same verdict in the two cases. In fact, the jury overwhelmingly concluded that the two cases were so different that they required different verdicts. Eighty-nine percent voted "not guilty" in the first case versus 11 percent in the second! Nearly *all* thought that it was okay to steer the trolley onto the siding and save the lives of the five at the expense of the life of the man on the siding. Almost *no one* thought it was okay to push the portly man into the path of the trolley to save the five. And the jurors' decisions were remarkably similar, regardless of the gender, age, education level, ethnicity, nationality, or—most interestingly—*whether they had been exposed to moral philosophy.* The obvious question is: "Why such disparate verdicts?"

Fortunately, the members of the jury were asked after the trial to justify the difference in their verdicts. Remember that the prosecuting attorney speculated that most jurors would agree that their conclusions should be based on a chain of *reasoning.* Well, in point of fact, that is not at all the way the actual jury arrived at their decisions. Only a small minority based their justification of the disparate verdicts for Clara and Frank on moral reasoning. That is, only a minority cited what they saw as a factual difference between the two cases and then argued that the two sets of facts led them down two different paths of moral reasoning.

Of the small number who used any moral reasoning at all, some cited the fact that Clara *foresaw* the death of the man on the siding as she pulled the switch, but Frank *intended* the death of the portly man. Put another way, Clara did not *use* the death of the man on the track to save the five; Frank did use the heavyset man in that way. This distinction is part of the so-called Principle of Double Effect, first set forth by St. Thomas Aquinas: An act to

ST. THOMAS AQUINAS (1225–1274)

Thomas was born in the Kingdom of Naples to Landulf, Count of Aquino, and Theodora, Countess of Teano. As a young man, he had an overwhelming desire to become a Dominican monk, but his family, who wanted him to become a Benedictine monk, held him prisoner in their castle for two years. Thomas ultimately prevailed and set off for the University of Paris.

The man who is now recognized as the premier Catholic philosopher and theologian of all time actually failed his first theological disputation and became known to his fellow students as "the dumb ox." He thereby became the informal patron saint of students who get off to a rough start in their freshman year.

Thomas went on to do what no philosopher or theologian writing today would dare to do: write a summa, or comprehensive systematic treatment of all philosophy and theology. In fact he wrote two of them: *Summa Theologiae* and *Summa Contra Gentiles*.

His *Summa Theologiae* runs the gamut from arguments for the existence of God to the development of good habits. One small plank in this "cathedral of thought" is his treatment of the ethical question of when it is permissible to perform an act that has both good and bad consequences. His answer, known as the Principle of Double Effect, is complex and subtle enough to demand its own chapter, The Bishop's Brief, page 63.

be morally good may have bad effects as a by-product, but bad means must not be used *to bring about* a good end.

Some others in the small group who used moral reasoning hung their differentiation of the two verdicts on the fact that Clara's act was impersonal, while Frank's act was personal. Presumably, what they meant was that Clara did not lay hands on the anonymous man on the siding, but Frank did lay hands on the heavyset gentleman.

Still others in this group cited the fact that Clara redirected an existing threat (the threat of being killed by a trolley), while Frank introduced a new threat (the threat of being pushed off the bridge).

Ladies and gentlemen of the jury, any one of these chains of reasoning is arguably sufficient to distinguish the case of Clara from the case of Frank (as well as, we shall soon see, from the case of Dr. Mapes). The prosecution's position rests on the argument that the case of Daphne Jones is analogous to a case that is, in actuality, totally unlike it in very significant ways. It is therefore entirely reasonable to find Daphne Jones not guilty on the utilitarian ground that killing one is better than killing five, while at the same time finding Dr. Mapes guilty of murder in a case in which the facts differ so significantly. For the case of Dr. Mapes, like the case of Frank, involves an intentional (versus a foreseen) bad effect; a personal (versus impersonal) action; and the introduction of a new threat (versus the redirection of an existing threat). All of these factors justify the simple application of a utilitarian principle in the case of Daphne Jones but not in the case of Dr. Mapes, and there is no logical inconsistency in judging the two cases differently.

But here's the topper. You will remember that in distinguishing between the two verdicts, only a small minority cited rational considerations at all; the huge majority of the jury used no moral reasoning whatsoever. Some of them simply reported that they had used utilitarian grounds—saving the greater number—in the case of Clara, and "deontological," rights-and-duties grounds in the case of Frank and the portly man, without attempting to reconcile the two approaches. Others said they based their disparate verdicts simply on intuition. They made comments like "I don't know how to explain it," or "It just seemed reasonable," or "It struck me that way," or "It was a gut feeling."

So District Attorney Cunningham's argument fails in two ways. He implies that a consistent utilitarianism would create a slippery slope from Daphne's pulling of the switch to Dr. Mapes's harvesting the organs of Bob Titherington and that both should therefore be condemned. But many jurors in the cases of Clara and Frank found real differences between them that made it rationally justifiable to decide the first case on the grounds of the greatest good for the greatest number while deciding the second case on a totally different basis. Moreover, the *majority* of this other jury

The huge majority of the jury used no moral reasoning whatsoever.

didn't use moral reasoning at all, so the question of explicit ethical consistency was moot for them. It was sufficient for these jurors that the two cases *felt* very different. And, in the end, for most of us, isn't that what the deciding factor in Daphne's case comes down to? Whether we can name it or not, we *feel* a difference between Daphne's case and the case of Dr. Mapes. We need not be embarrassed by deciding Daphne's case on the basis of how it feels. Philosophers even give that method a fancy name: ethical intuitionism.

In summary, then, common sense has again been proven right, as it almost always is. Copernicus's theory that it is the Earth that moves around the sun is one of those rare exceptions that prove the rule! *That's* why history remembers him!

Daphne Jones has done nothing wrong. Her utilitarian approach in deciding to throw the switch is uncomplicated by the extra factors we have found in the case of Dr. Mapes or in the case of Frank and the portly man. Like the jury in the cases of Clara and Frank, you must not be duped by the false analogy drawn by District Attorney Cunningham between two very different cases. You must find Daphne Jones not guilty of manslaughter.

THE PROFESSOR'S ANALYSIS

////////////////////////////

Critical Thinking in Contemporary Life

THE NEW SCHOOL
New York
Friday, April 19, 2013

Good evening, everyone. Since they switched our room, just let me make sure everyone's in the right place. This is Lifelong Learning 103, Critical Thinking in Contemporary Life. Anyone here for the Nineteenth-Century Russian Novel? Yes? That's been moved downstairs—to room 21, I think. If it's not there, try room 23.

So . . . I'm Kiara James, and for the next eight weeks we'll be trying to sharpen our critical-thinking skills and use them to analyze contemporary issues. Tonight, for instance, we'll be looking at the trial that seems to have the whole nation in a tizzy, the case of Daphne Jones and the runaway trolley.

But before we get to the trial, we have a lot of work to do. We're going to hone our thinking skills so that we can, hopefully, take a more intelligent look at the questions raised by the trial. There's been a lot of commentary on the trial, from PBS to the Drudge Report, and some of it has been pretty smart, but a lot of it hasn't.

Has anyone here been exposed to any philosophy courses? Okay, I see a few hands, but overall I'd say most of you have not. Which is fine. It's not something you need to have in order to succeed at critical thinking. By the end of this course, you will all be more critical thinkers.

Tonight, we're going to start off by taking a look at analogies and the role they play in how we think about things. Then we'll examine the role analogy has played in the trolley trial. Someone want to define *analogy* for us? Yes?

It's a comparison of two things. Like, "You're pretty as a picture."

Thank you. Not for saying I'm pretty as a picture, although I thank you for that, too. But you're right. An analogy is a comparison. The example you used, "pretty as a picture," compares a person (who, I'll admit, may or may not be me) to a picture—in terms of prettiness.

That's a fairly specific analogy, because it says up front what criterion you're using to compare—let's just say, *me*—to a picture. You're speaking specifically of our comparative prettiness.

But analogies generally compare two things or two people or two events without telling us exactly what the point of comparison is. Any examples?

Before his injury, Derek Jeter was like a jackrabbit.

Yes. Others?

At his news conference, President Obama was like a sphinx.

Yes.

These analogies leave it vague as to exactly how Derek Jeter was like a jackrabbit. Was it his ears? Probably not. Was it his love life? Hopefully not. The reference was probably to his quickness or something like that, right?

How exactly was the president like a sphinx? Was it that they both reside in the Egyptian desert? Was it that they're both made of some kind of stone? Hmm, that one's trickier, right? Because the word *stone* may be used metaphorically, too, like "stony silence." But clearly, the point of the comparison isn't the mineral composition of their bodies. We're probably supposed to think that President Obama was inscrutable, or something of the sort.

So analogies are used to compare two things that are alike in some ways but different in others. Suppose we say, "An apple is like a pear." We can think of lots of ways an apple is, in fact, like a pear, right? Let's put some on the board.

They're both fruits.

They're a similar size.

They both taste good.

Okay . . . let's stop there, before this becomes a home ec class. Now let's list some ways in which they're different. Any suggestions?

Color. Apples are generally red or partly red—but not always, I guess, since Granny Smiths are bright green—and pears are generally yellow or brownish or light green, but not always those, either. I guess there's some overlap in color between apples and pears.

Right, but in general, as you say, apples and pears are dissimilar in color. So you wouldn't say someone was apple-cheeked if you meant her cheeks were yellow or brownish or light green, like a pear. Other points of dissimilarity?

Apples are fairly round, and pears are, uh, well, pear shaped.

Whoa, let's stop right there, because you've stumbled across an important point about analogies. When you said, in effect, that the shape of a pear is like the shape of a pear, the reason you and the rest of us laughed is that it is, in a sense, a *perfect* analogy. That is, the shape of a pear *is* like the shape of a pear—in *every possible way.* An analogy doesn't get any better than that, right? Wrong.

Paradoxically, a "perfect" analogy is a lousy analogy.

Paradoxically, a "perfect" analogy is a lousy analogy. It doesn't give us any new information about the shape of a pear. Notice that this isn't just because the two things being compared are represented by identical words. That's an extreme case. But "That hexagon is like a six-sided figure" doesn't tell us anything new about that hexagon (assuming we already know the definition of *hexagon*). That is, it might tell us something about the word *hexagon*, but it doesn't tell us anything about *that* hexagon.

So now we know that a perfect analogy isn't a good analogy. So what? What's the point of all this hair-splitting? That's a good question and one that philosophers have spent a lot of time thinking about. Contemporary philosophers, especially those in the English-speaking world, have gotten a bad rap for making hair-splitting distinctions in language and logic, rather than writing about the "big questions," like the ones Paul Gauguin used as a title for his painting in 1897, *Where Do We Come From? What Are We? Where Are We Going?* Some people think that today's British and American philosophers are sort of diddling while Rome burns, if you will. Some of you may feel that way about today's discussion of analogies. I won't ask for a show of hands.

On the other hand, I hope you'll agree by the end of this course that it is very important to hone the *tools* we use to ask questions and make decisions. Otherwise, we may not have a shot at making a *good* decision. The tools of critical thinking are language and logic.

Is sharpening the axe as important as cutting down the tree? Obviously not. But without a sharp axe, you may not do a good job of cutting down the tree. You may even fail to cut it down at all. Is studying the use of language and logic as important as answering Gauguin's questions? Of course not, but without a clear sense of how to use those tools, we may come up with lousy answers. Hey, I just made an analogy! How about that?

So why does our analysis of analogies matter? It matters because we learned that analogies always compare two things that are sort of alike and sort of different. This makes analogies both very useful *and* very dangerous. Analogies are a two-edged sword, to use another analogy! The danger in using analogies is that people often argue that because two things are similar in one respect, they must also be similar in another respect, when in fact the two things may not be similar at all in the second respect.

But who cares? What difference does it make in the real world? Well, let's try to apply what we've discussed today to some real issues that are in the news. Before we get to the trolley trial, can anyone think of another news story that involves an analogy?

Yeah. How about the controversy over teaching Intelligent Design in public schools as an alternative to the theory of evolution?

Great example. Where do you see an analogy?

Well, I guess the argument for Intelligent Design is that there are a lot of intricate things in nature. The example they often use is the human eyeball. The amazing complexity of such a thing seems a lot like the intricacy of some man-made things—for example, the iPhone. So we can assume there must have been a Steve Jobs type in the sky who designed the eyeball.

Good. Not surprisingly, in the philosophy of religion, that's called the argument from analogy. How many of you buy that argument? Looks like about half of you. How many don't? About the same number, I'd say. How many aren't sure what to think? A few.

There are two ways in which an argument from analogy can fail to be convincing. The first is that the similarity of the two things may not be all that persuasive. In the eighteenth century, there was a version of the Intelligent Design argument making the rounds, which said, "The universe is like a giant clock." (This was shortly after the time of Isaac Newton, and mechanical explanations of the universe were in the air.) "When we see a clock," they said, "we conclude there must have been a clockmaker. Likewise, when we ponder the universe, we

INTELLIGENT DESIGN

The Discovery Institute, a conservative think tank established in 1990, adopted the term *Intelligent Design* to designate the theory that "certain features of the universe and of living things are best explained by an intelligent cause, not an undirected process such as natural selection." The institute advocated teaching intelligent design alongside, and as a rival to, the theory of evolution in public schools. Opponents quickly claimed that to do so would introduce Judeo-Christian religious doctrine into the curriculum in violation of the "establishment clause" of the First Amendment to the U.S. Constitution, which has generally been interpreted to mandate the separation of church and state.

The institute claims that Intelligent Design is an evidence-based scientific theory, not a religious doctrine. It is not, they say, the same as creationism, because it does not spell out exactly who or what this intelligent cause was, nor does it insist that the process must have happened exactly as the biblical book of Genesis tells it.

On the basis of this distinction from creationism, the institute has argued that teaching Intelligent Design does not violate the Constitution. In the U.S. District Court case, *Kitzmiller v. Dover (PA) Area School District*, however, the court ruled that Intelligent Design is religion rather than science, and the teaching of it in public schools is therefore unconstitutional.

must conclude that there was a Divine Clockmaker or, if you will, a Creator." The Scottish philosopher David Hume asked, "Why do you say the universe is like a clock, of all things? Couldn't you just as well say that the universe is like a giant animal, constantly in motion, with all its parts working harmoniously together? Would you then conclude that a 'mother' universe must have given birth to the current one because that's what happens in the animal realm?"

So one reason an argument from analogy might fail to be convincing is that the supposed point of similarity of the two things may not be all that obvious. *How* similar is an eyeball, after all, to an iPhone? Isn't it more similar to the specialized light-sensitive cells of a mollusk, which some Intelligent Design advocates are willing to concede did come about through natural selection?

How similar is an eyeball, after all, to an iPhone?

The other way an argument from analogy may fail to be convincing is that the two things being compared—the eyeball and the iPhone—may in fact be persuasively similar in one or more respects, but that doesn't necessarily mean that the two things are also similar in another respect: in this case, how they came into being. Just because the iPhone was created by Apple doesn't mean the eyeball didn't develop in a completely different way: for example, over millions of years through random mutation and natural selection. What caused the two things to come into being may be one of their points of *dis*similarity. Maybe Steve Jobs was influenced or even inspired by the intricacy of natural things, I don't know. But that could have happened regardless of how those natural things came into existence.

Okay, reality check. Of the people who found the Intelligent Design argument convincing a few minutes ago, how many find it less so now? Uh-huh, a few. Of the people who weren't sure what to think about it before, how many now find it definitely unpersuasive? Okay, another few. That's an example of the effect of having sharp tools with which to make decisions. All we did was look at the nature of analogies and analyze how they might be used to mislead others or ourselves, and, as a result, some of us changed our minds about a real issue in the real world. Not all of us, but, rightly or wrongly, some did. Maybe

DAVID HUME (1711–1776)

Born in Edinburgh, Hume was raised by his widowed mother. He once described himself as "a man of mild Dispositions, of Command of Temper, of an open, social, and cheerful Humour, capable of Attachment, but little susceptible of Enmity, and of great Moderation in all my passions." It was this mild-mannered man who, Kant said, woke him from his "dogmatic slumber"!

Hume was the most important of the British empiricists, thinkers who maintained that philosophy cannot go beyond what is given to us in sensory experience. He was skeptical, for example, about the notion of cause and effect. When one billiard ball strikes another and the second ball moves, all we can really conclude from our experience, he said, is that the two events constantly occur together, not that there is some necessary causal connection between them.

His skepticism extended to what he called "Natural Religion," that is, religion that attempts to base knowledge of the super-natural world on some quality of the natural world, such as its intricacy or its beauty. One of the Natural Religion arguments that Hume refuted was the argument from analogy, also known as the argument from design, an eighteenth-century forerunner of Intelligent Design.

those of you who are still of the same opinion suspect that I "dazzled you with bullshit." That's what a student last semester told me. Maybe I fogged your minds and tried to put one over on you. That's okay, if you think that. Skepticism is good. But even if I did try to trick you, it would only be an argument for sharpening *your* critical-thinking skills so I and people of my ilk don't bamboozle you. Because, make no mistake, there are lots of folks out there—politicians, lawyers, salesmen—who are trying to do just that.

Okay, after all that, we're finally ready to take a look at the trolley trial. How has analogy been employed in the trial? Yes?

The prosecution is trying to say that Daphne's throwing the switch to save five people while killing one is analogous to a surgeon's removing the vital organs from a healthy person in order to save five critically injured people.

Good. The prosecution's case rests totally on an analogy. But note that the defense's case also relies heavily on analogies. The defense lawyer says Daphne's case (let's call it Case A) is strongly analogous to another case in which a woman *driving* a trolley made a similar choice to allow one to be killed in order to save five (Case B). Next, the defense lawyer argues that the case of the surgeon (Case C) is strongly analogous to that of a man who stopped a trolley by throwing a very heavy man in front of it to save five people on the track (Case D). And then the defense lawyer concludes that because A is strongly analogous to B, and C is strongly analogous to D, and a prior jury already decided that B and D are *not* strongly analogous, therefore we should conclude that A and C are not strongly analogous, either!

Whew! Everybody with us? Let's take it one step at a time. The defense attorney has argued:

(1) Case A is strongly analogous to Case B. The case of throwing the switch is strongly analogous to the case of driving the trolley.

(2) Case C is strongly analogous to Case D. The case of the surgeon is strongly analogous to the case of throwing the man off the bridge.

(3) Case B is *not* strongly analogous to Case D. The case of driving the trolley is *not* strongly analogous to the case of throwing the man off the bridge.

(4) Therefore, Case A is not strongly analogous to Case C. The case of throwing the switch is not strongly analogous to the case of the surgeon.

Wow, look at the complicated use of analogies here. We've already seen that analogies can sometimes be misleading, so the possibility of being misled by this convoluted case is enormous.

So what are the questions you would want to ask about the analogies the lawyers have used in this case? Let's confine ourselves to the prosecution's analogy between Daphne's pulling the switch and Dr. Mapes's harvesting of a healthy patient's organs.

The questions I would ask are the same questions we asked about the eyeball and the iPhone. The first ones are, "How similar are the two cases, really? Is Daphne's pulling the switch really all that similar to taking vital organs from a healthy person, just because they both involve the death of one person in exchange for saving five?"

Right. We know that analogies always compare two things that are alike in some ways and different in others, so the question is, as you say, whether the two cases are really all *that* similar. It's hard to think of two things that aren't analogous in *some* way. Lewis Carroll, the British logician who wrote *Alice in Wonderland*, tried and came up with "How is a writing desk like a raven?" but somebody had an answer: "Poe wrote on them."

So the next question is whether any of the differences between the two cases actually make *a difference. Even if we think the two cases are strongly similar, do any of the ways they are different lead us to think that Dr. Mapes is guilty of a crime but Daphne may not be?*

Bingo!

Okay. I'll leave you to ponder these questions. It will be interesting to see how the jury decides them next week.

THE PSYCHOLOGIST'S OPINION

///////////////////////////

"A Travesty of Justice"

Irving Wattenberg, Ph.D., Editor-in-Chief

PSYCHOLOGY NOW!
The Magazine of Human Behavior, online edition
Friday, April 19, 2013

Much of the American public has been transfixed in the past few weeks by the television coverage of the so-called trolley trial of Daphne Jones, now being argued before the Court of Public Opinion. Questions of moral and legal responsibility have become hot topics in the media and at the water cooler, as the two sides have debated whether—and under what circumstances—it is defensible to allow the loss of life of one person in order to save more lives. Unfortunately, the controversy shows that neither side understands the scientific basis of moral judgments.

It has now been demonstrated convincingly by functional Magnetic Resonance Imaging (fMRI) that in certain types of moral dilemmas, the parts of the brain associated with emotions play a far greater role in determining our moral judgments than do the parts of the brain associated with cognitive activity. This is particularly true in cases involving *personal* violations of another human being (say, harvesting a man's vital organs or throwing him off a bridge) rather than *impersonal* violations (say, Daphne Jones's pulling the switch that diverted a trolley toward another person whom she did not know).

In short, we human beings make the moral judgments we do because we are hardwired that way. Our repugnance at the thought of killing someone with our bare hands (or with a scalpel or by pushing him off a bridge) is related to our fear of *being* deliberately killed by another human being. If we were as acutely aware of the chance of someone's diverting a trolley to run us over—if that were an everyday occurrence in our community—we would presumably have a strong emotional response to that possibility as well, and we might feel differently about Daphne's action. But the fact of the matter is that we do not have such an emotional reaction to what Daphne did, and it is inappropriate to judge her as if we did.

It is understandable that in the prescientific world, philosophers looked for a moral reason as to why it is better to play an impersonal role in someone's dying than it is to

We human beings make the moral judgments we do because we are hardwired that way.

kill him. In today's scientific world, we look to psychological facts rather than moral value judgments to reach our conclusions. It is a matter of *fact* that we have an emotional repugnance to Dr. Mapes's act; it is a matter of *fact* that we do not have a similar emotional repugnance to Daphne's. The similarities the prosecutor sees in the two cases are ones he arrived at *cognitively.* From an *emotional* standpoint, the two cases could not be more dissimilar. In so-called moral decisions, emotion always trumps reason.

We can speculate that the vast importance of emotion in "personal," hands-on acts of killing stems from human evolution: that is, from natural selection. Here's the way it might work. Societies made up of individuals with brains genetically programmed to have a stronger emotional aversion to deliberately killing one another were the societies more likely to survive, for obvious reasons. Because they were more likely to survive, their genes make up the greater share of today's gene pool. For this reason, almost all people living today have a genetic predisposition to have an emotional aversion to killing another human being in a "personal" way.

But that's not all. At a cultural level, the societies that survived were likely to pass on to their children customs and mores based on the genetic, emotional predispositions of the parents. This adds yet another level to their descendants' emotional aversion to killing: the maelstrom of emotions caused by breaking a cultural taboo. Taboos—the strongest, most emotionally loaded negative rules in a society—developed because of the insecurity of individuals living in a dangerous world. Societies in which the emotional areas of the brains of its members were most sensitive to the dangers of being an individual are the societies in which the strongest groupthink (i.e., taboos) developed. These are also the societies more likely to survive. Most people living today therefore have both a genetic, emotional aversion to "personal" killing and a genetic, emotional aversion to breaking societal taboos, such as the one about personal killing.

When faced with a less personal decision to allow a death—like Daphne Jones's decision to throw the switch—we are more likely to use the parts of our brain associated with cognition. We come up with an abstract principle: Killing one is better than killing five. Because our emotions are not in conflict with that principle, we are likely to adopt it.

Cognitively, it might seem that Daphne's case is similar to the case of the rogue surgeon or the man who threw another man to his death: In both cases, one was sacrificed to save five. But psychologically and emotionally, there is a huge difference between Daphne's case and the other two. As a matter of plain fact, the jury should—and almost certainly will—find Daphne Jones not guilty.

COMMENTS

eddieinbrooklyn

Your editorial seems inconsistent to me. It is peppered with value judgments: "The jury *should* find Daphne not guilty."

"It is *inappropriate* to behave as we would if we had an emotional reaction to Daphne's pulling the switch." At the same time, you want to say that all value judgments are reducible to the way we are emotionally hardwired. If that is so, why do you need to say that the jury *shouldn't* find Daphne guilty? They either will or they won't. If they do find her guilty, would you then conclude that they were emotionally hardwired to do so? You want to say that what we call values are just a particular kind of fact—hardwired, emotional fact—but you try to sneak some values in the back door.

cutiepie137

You're missing the point, **eddie**. It's precisely *because* values are reducible to facts that the jury should find her not guilty. If they find her guilty, it will be because they think there's some reason they "should." But there isn't. They will find her guilty only if the prosecution succeeds in confusing them. I think we probably agree that decisions shouldn't be based on confusion.

nerdyferdy##

Cutiepie's right, **eddie**. There's no such thing as moral

philosophy anymore, now that we have psychology and neu-
roscience. All those centuries that philosophers *speculated*
about why we *should* see the world their way—those days
are gone. Now we know from scientific studies of the brain
that those philosophical ideas were just brain farts like any
other nonscientific idea. Get with the 21st century, **eddie**.

---

eddieinbrooklyn

Whoa. You guys are running around in circles. What do
you mean, "There's no such thing as moral philosophy anymore?" As a statement of *fact,* that's obviously not true. What
you're actually saying is "There *shouldn't* be such a thing as
moral philosophy anymore." That's a value judgment. And
cutiepie's making a value judgment when she says jury
decisions shouldn't be based on confusion. I agree with her,
but let's call it what it is—a value judgment. Anyway, my real
point is that Dr. Wattenberg in the editorial is in effect saying
that we *should* make moral and legal decisions on the basis
of our emotional reactions. That's his *value* judgment about
the role emotion *should* play. He's not just saying that emotion does in *fact* play a prominent role in our moral decisions.
Who could disagree with that? But he's also saying that, as

far as he's concerned, that's the *proper* way to make such decisions. He's now left the world of facts and is making a value judgment about what's proper.

---

professorkgw

Eddie is telling you guys that you're committing something called the naturalistic fallacy. The British philosopher G. E. Moore said the word "good" is indefinable. It isn't reducible to any "natural" quality, like, say, "pleasurable." By "natural" he meant "factual": something that can be observed and measured by a scientist. There are scientific tests as to whether something is pleasurable, but there aren't any scientific tests as to whether something is good. So, even if it is a *fact* that we have an emotional predisposition to disapprove the "personal" killing of Dr. Mapes's patient and do not in *fact* have such a predisposition to disapprove Daphne's pulling the switch, that doesn't mean that we must necessarily find the one bad and the other good.

Think of it this way: If someone were to claim that "good" means "pleasurable," would she understand what I meant if I asked her, "But is something that's pleasurable necessarily good?" Of course she'd understand me! She wouldn't think

G. E. MOORE (1873–1958)

George Edward Moore was born in the London suburbs, one of eight children. As a child, he was educated mostly by his parents, his father teaching him reading, writing, and music, and his mother teaching him French. At the age of eighteen, he went off to Cambridge University to study classics, but he soon came under the influence of Bertrand Russell and added philosophy to his studies.

He reportedly hated the name George Edward and began to sign himself "G. E." His wife, for reasons best known to herself, called him "Bill."

Moore was known for his commonsense approach to all branches of philosophy. In his ethics, for example, he argued for the indefinability of "good" by quoting Bishop Joseph Butler's famous statement, "Everything is what it is and not another thing." Moore's main argument for the naturalistic fallacy is basically "Good is good and not something else."

By turning philosophy away from grand pronouncements on the nature of the world or how we should behave and toward analysis of what we mean, Moore, along with other British philosophers like Russell and Wittgenstein, set the course for Anglo-American philosophy in the twentieth and twenty-first centuries.

I was asking, "Is something that's pleasurable necessarily *pleasurable*?" That's because we all know that "good" is in a whole different realm from the world of scientific facts. It's a term of value. So even if we do, in fact, have a genetic predisposition—or just a psychological predisposition—to find hands-on killing repugnant, we can always ask whether we *should* base our moral and legal judgments on that fact.

---

mixedupinaustin

Hey, this is a good discussion! And by "good," I mean "fun."

---

professorkgw

You're right, **mixedup**, even though you did just commit the naturalistic fallacy.

---

mixedupinaustin

There are worse things, right?

THE BISHOP'S BRIEF

////////////////////////////

Amicus Curiae Brief

*Bishop Pedro O'Shaughnessey,
on behalf of the United States Conference
of Catholic Bishops*

Friday, April 19, 2013

Ladies and gentlemen of the jury of the Court of
Public Opinion, as the bishop of the Roman Catholic
Diocese of Huntington, West Virginia, and a canon lawyer, I submit this Friend of the Court brief on behalf of
the United States Conference of Catholic Bishops to advocate for the acquittal of Daphne Jones. The brief will be
based on the Roman Catholic Church's teaching on the
Principle of Double Effect.

The history of this principle began in the thirteenth
century, when St. Thomas Aquinas set it forth in his

Summa Theologiae as an argument for the permissibility of killing another person in self-defense.

The catechism of the Catholic Church teaches that our basic moral principle should be to pursue good and avoid that which is evil. But St. Thomas points out that an action often has *two* effects, one good and one bad, and under certain conditions it may be permissible to perform a good act that has a bad consequence, *even one that we would ordinarily be obligated to avoid.* And so, while killing another person is generally prohibited, killing in self-defense is sometimes permissible.

Under certain conditions it may be permissible to perform a good act that has a bad consequence, even one that we would ordinarily be obligated to avoid.

St. Thomas posits that saving one's own life is generally a good thing, "seeing that it is natural to everything to keep itself in 'being,' as far as possible." The problem, of course, is that in the act of killing in self-defense, one must purchase one's own continued "being" at the price of discontinuing someone else's. Still, St. Thomas argues that under certain, very specific conditions, it is permissible to cause the bad effect alongside the good. His conditions, as further elaborated by the Catholic Church, are fourfold:

(1) The act itself must be morally good or at least indifferent.

(2) The agent may not positively will the bad effect but may permit it. If he could attain the good effect without the bad effect, he should do so.

(3) The good effect must flow from the action at least as directly as the bad effect. In other words, the good effect must be produced directly by the action, not by the bad effect. Otherwise the agent would be using a bad means to a good end, which is never allowed.

(4) The good effect must be sufficiently desirable to compensate for the allowing of the bad effect.

I will now apply these criteria to a case that is unrelated to self-defense, that of Daphne Jones:

(1) If we separate the action from all of its consequences, the act of diverting a trolley is morally neutral, so condition 1 is met.

(2) Ms. Jones did not, as far as we know, *will* the death of the man on the siding, Mr. Chet Farley. She merely *foresaw* and *permitted* Mr. Farley's death as a side effect of saving the five people. We must all surely grant that if Ms. Jones could have saved the five without causing the death of Mr. Farley, she would have done so. Condition 2 is met.

(3) Ms. Jones, in throwing the switch, did not first kill Mr. Farley and then use his body to stop the trolley. No, the immediate, direct effect of throwing the switch was the saving of the five. Only later (though admittedly only a few seconds later) did the trolley (and not the throwing of the switch) kill Mr. Farley. Condition 3 is met.

(4) The goodness of saving five lives does outweigh the loss of one. Condition 4 is met.

The prosecution makes much of the supposed analogy to the case of Dr. Mapes, who killed a healthy patient by harvesting his organs to save five other patients. But the case of Dr. Mapes does not meet the four criteria contained in the Principle of Double Effect:

(1) The act of killing an innocent person is not in itself a good act, so condition 1 is apparently not met. (But see the discussion of condition 3 below.)

(2) It would seem that Dr. Mapes must have willed the death of patient #6, Mr. Bob Titherington, since he knew that removing his vital organs was tantamount to killing him. Therefore, condition 2 would not be met. (But see the discussion of condition 3 below.)

(3) Condition 3 is the nub of the matter. Some would argue that the "act" Dr. Mapes committed was not the *killing* of Mr. Titherington, but rather the *removal of his organs;* Mr. Titherington's death was merely an unintended side effect of having his organs removed. By this line of reasoning, Dr. Mapes's case is allegedly analogous to that of Ms. Jones. That is to say, Dr. Mapes was attempting to perform an act with a good consequence (the saving of five patients' lives) and a bad consequence (Mr. Titherington's death). Condition 1 would supposedly be met, because the act of

removing organs is itself good or at least indifferent (though one might counterargue that removing *healthy* organs is never a good or even indifferent act). Condition 2 would supposedly be met, because Dr. Mapes never directly willed the death of Mr. Titherington, only the procurement of his vital organs.

It is here that we see the genius of condition 3 and why Dr. Mapes's case fails to meet it. Condition 3 was created precisely to counteract the sophistry of making too-fine distinctions, such as that between the act of removing vital organs and the act of killing. Note that condition 3 says that the good effect must flow from the action *at least as directly* as the bad effect. So, even if one says that Dr. Mapes's *act* was merely the removal of Mr. Titherington's organs, the fact is that the bad effect (Mr. Titherington's death) followed that act immediately. The good effect, the saving of five patients' lives, followed several minutes afterward. Therefore, Dr. Mapes was, in effect, using a bad means (the act of harvesting, along with its *immediate* consequence, Mr. Titherington's death) to a good end, which is never permissible.

We are willing to concede that Dr. Mapes's case may meet condition 4. The good effect arguably did outweigh the bad effect.

Now, let's look at the broader context of the Principle of Double Effect. The Catholic Church's position on abortion, for instance, rests in part on this principle.

Performing an abortion to save the life of the mother is not permissible, because it does not meet either condition 1 or condition 2. The act of killing an innocent person is not good in itself, and doing it to save the mother's life, while that would certainly be a desirable effect, would require using a bad effect, the death of the fetus, as a means by which to achieve the good effect.

If, however, the pregnant woman was diagnosed with cancer of the uterus, it would be permissible to perform a hysterectomy, even though that would end the life of the fetus, because performing the operation meets all four conditions of the Principle of Double Effect:

(1) Removing cancerous tissue is good in itself.

(2) Neither the woman nor the surgeon *wills* the death of the fetus; they merely foresee it and permit it.

(3) It is the hysterectomy rather than the death of the fetus that saves the woman's life.

(4) Saving the mother's life is at least as great a good as saving the life of the fetus.

Another example of the church's use of the Principle of Double Effect is in the issue of assisted suicide. Helping a patient to kill himself is never permissible under Catholic teaching, because it violates the commandment not to kill. In other words, it does not meet condition 1. It will not do to say that the physician is only providing a drug, rather than directly killing the patient, because his *intent* is to kill the patient (condition 2). If the physician says that his intent is merely to "end the patient's suffering," it is still the case that it is the patient's death (the bad effect) that brings about the good effect of relieving the patient's pain. Condition 3 is not met.

So, may a physician prescribe large doses of morphine to a patient for pain control, even though that much morphine will in all probability hasten the death of the patient? Yes. Why?

Condition 1: Controlling a patient's pain is good in itself.

Condition 2: The physician does not will the death of the patient; she wills the cessation of pain, even though she *foresees* and *permits* the probable hastening of death.

Condition 3: The relief of the pain (good effect) is not *caused* by the bad effect (the patient's death). In fact, the relief of pain will precede the patient's death. Contrast this with the motives of Dr. Kevorkian, who presumably assisted in the administration of a life-ending drug because he wanted the patient's death to cause the cessation of his suffering.

Condition 4: The good effect of relieving *unbearable* pain does outweigh the bad effect of hastening the patient's death. (It would not be permissible, however, to give life-threatening doses of morphine to, say, relieve an ordinary headache.)

To return to the case of Daphne Jones, it is the position of the U.S. Conference of Catholic Bishops that Ms. Jones did nothing worse than the surgeon who removes the uterus of a pregnant woman with uterine cancer or the doctor who prescribes life-threatening doses of morphine to a patient in severe pain. The jury should therefore find Ms. Jones not guilty.

In conclusion, I would like to address a subsidiary issue. Many critics of church teachings on matters such as abortion accuse the church of "hair-splitting." We would only point out that making fine distinctions in borderline cases is an unavoidable consequence of making *any* moral (or legal) rule. Whenever a moral (or legal) line is drawn, there will always be cases close to the line; the task of the church (or the court) then becomes to decide which side of the line they fall on. The church has been unfairly criticized for making too-fine distinctions. In a similar way, the teachings of the Talmud have been ridiculed for their specificity. In response, we would ask the jury to consider that the case they have been asked to decide rests precisely on such fine distinctions. Indeed, the very reason we have juries is to make such distinctions. Otherwise, a computer could apply the penal code to individual cases.

I thank the court for the opportunity to present this Friend of the Court brief.

THE ALTRUIST'S DILEMMA

////////////////////////

NPR Debates

NATIONAL PUBLIC RADIO
Saturday, April 20, 2013

Good afternoon, ladies and gentlemen, and welcome
to *NPR Debates,* the show in which selected listeners meet to
debate pressing issues of the day. I'm your host, Jeff Salaby.

Two weeks ago, our debaters argued both sides of *The
People v. Daphne Jones,* the so-called runaway trolley trial.
In the following days, we received an unusual avalanche of
mail from you, our listeners. Many of your letters attempted
to apply moral principles from various religious traditions to
the issues raised by the trial. In particular, a number of listeners sought to apply the Golden Rule: "Do unto others as
you would have others do unto you." These responses were
from, of course, Christians, but also from Jews, Muslims,
Hindus, Confucianists, Buddhists, and Baha'is, who cited
a version of the Golden Rule from their own scriptures.

As we looked through all of these letters, we noticed a curious phenomenon: Some of them argued for the acquittal of Ms. Jones on the grounds that they themselves would not want to be punished for a well-intended act such as pulling the switch to divert the trolley. Others argued for acquittal because they would want to be treated as she treated the five people whom she saved. Still others argued for convicting Ms. Jones because they would not want to be treated as the innocent man on the siding was treated.

So it appeared that the Golden Rule was ambiguous when applied to deciding the guilt or innocence of Ms. Jones. That got some of our more diabolical minds here at *NPR Debates* to thinking about how to frame a scenario in which the application of the Golden Rule was less ambiguous.

Leonard, it's time to read the scenario!

Thanks, Jeff. Here's what we came up with:

You are on the siding, tied to the track. You see the out-of-control trolley careering toward the five people on the main track. By contorting your body, you can reach the switch with your foot and divert the trolley onto the siding, killing you, but saving the five. Do you flip the switch?

Okay, thanks, Leonard. Hmm, did anyone else's pulse rate just go up? I know mine did.

So the question on the docket today is: Is altruism always good? Here to debate that question, as it relates to our scenario, are listeners Marv Feldman from Rochester, Minnesota, and Stella Rotelli from Atlanta, Georgia. Marv and Stella were chosen based on the content of their letters. After the debate, we'll ask the audience to comment on whether it shed any light on the issues raised in the actual runaway trolley trial.

Marv and Stella, welcome to you both. Each of you will present your case in five minutes, and then there will be an opportunity for a two-minute rebuttal. So, Marv, you lead off. Tell us why we should always behave altruistically.

Thanks, Jeff. Well, the first point I'd like to make is something you alluded to in the introduction. If most of the major religions of the world think it's good to treat others the way we would want to be treated, surely that's evidence that it's a good rule. If only one religion valued altruism, we might wonder whether it was really ancient wisdom or just some airy-fairy idealism. But it seems to be a value shared by most, if not all, of the major religions. Could they all be wrong? Sure. But I don't think so. I think it's more likely that the ancients were onto something important—that we're meant to look out for one another in this life—and that we self-centered modern types often blind ourselves to that truth.

The second point I'd like to make is that this new scenario in which I'm chained to the track seems to me to be very similar to the actual events that are the subject of the trial. The only difference is that in the new scenario, if I flip the switch, I'm also the one who pays the price. Now, I'm one who thinks that Daphne Jones is not guilty. I think she did the right thing by pulling the switch and sacrificing Mr. Farley in order to save the five people on the main track. But, if that's so, I don't see any reason why I should exempt myself from that calculation. If I was tied to the track on the siding and could still reach the switch, what possible moral argument could I give for not applying the kill-one-to-save-five rule? The truth is there is no such argument. Now, would I really pull the switch in that situation? I don't know. But the question of whether I *would* do it is a different question from whether I *should* do it, and I see no reason to let myself off the hook.

The third point I'd like to make I got off the Web when I Googled *altruism*. A Princeton University philosopher's name kept coming up, and he has made up some analogies about altruism that I find pretty convincing. And they speak to today's question: Is altruism *always* good?

I'm probably going to screw up his scenarios a little, but here goes. One of them runs something like this:

You're on your way to work, and you walk by a small pond. There's a little kid apparently

> **The question of whether I *would* do it is a different question from whether I *should* do it.**

playing in the water, which is only a few feet deep. When you get close enough to see better, you can tell that he's a *very* little guy, and he's not playing—he's flailing about in the water, unable to get his footing and about to go under. You look around for his parents, but they're nowhere in sight. It would be easy enough to wade in and help him out, but you have on a new pair of shoes that cost you three hundred dollars. They'll be ruined if you go in, and there clearly isn't time to take them off.

So the question is: Should I wade in or not? Well, now, really. Who of us would not enter the water to save the little guy?

Now, says this professor—Peter Singer is his name—think about this situation. Thousands of children in Third World countries die every day from diseases that could be prevented if they had access to clean drinking water. Giving three hundred dollars to Oxfam would go a long way toward providing clean drinking water for several children. Shouldn't you always send Oxfam the money you'd otherwise spend on luxury items like fancy shoes?

Or how about this one? A stranger in the subway station offers you enough money to buy that new plasma TV you've been thinking about. All you have to do is persuade a young street kid to follow this shady character into his car. You've been reading in the paper that a gang of petty crooks has been selling street kids to a "medical" outfit in Haiti, where they kill the kids and sell their organs to wealthy Americans who are waiting for organs. Sounds like Dr. Mapes from the Daphne Jones case, huh?

How many of us would take the money and buy the TV with a clear conscience? None of us, of course.

As it happens, like many middle-class Americans, I own a plasma TV. Singer says that any time any of us buys a luxury item in lieu of giving the money to a charity that provides street kids with the basic necessities of life, we are doing essentially the same thing as giving the kid over to the gangster.

So here's my argument for altruism. All of us have some of it. All of us would sacrifice ourselves some in some situations. It seems at some level to be a universal value. But if we're really honest with ourselves, we know we should be just as altruistic in analogous situations, including pulling the switch to save the five despite its causing our own demise. And we know down deep that the reason we aren't that altruistic in all situations is that we unconsciously or deliberately suppress what we know to be true: that the plight of others has a moral claim on us that we just don't want to face.

Thank you.

PETER SINGER (1946–)

Singer is an Australian utilitarian philosopher who teaches at Princeton University. He is probably best known for his 1975 book *Animal Liberation,* in which he argues for the ethical treatment of animals by extending Jeremy Bentham's principle of the greatest happiness for the greatest number to include nonhuman animals. Because of the cruelties of meat production, Singer is a vegetarian. He also refuses to wear leather.

Singer is almost equally well known for his provocative analogies in support of the notion that those who have more than they need should give to those who have less. His support for the elimination of poverty stems from his utilitarian concern for the greatest happiness for the greatest number.

Singer is always provocative. Among his many controversial views is his judgment that athletes should be allowed to take performance-enhancing drugs (as long as they are not harmed by them). Otherwise, he argues, the genetically best-endowed athletes have an unfair advantage.

Like Bentham, Singer has tried to directly influence public policy; he ran for the Australian Senate on the Greens ticket in 1996. Although his bid was unsuccessful, in 2005 *TIME* magazine named him one of the one hundred most influential people in the world.

All right, Marv. Excellent. You make a very compelling case. Stella, you've got a real challenge—making the case for *not* always being altruistic. What do you have for us?

Well, Jeff, I feel literally like the devil's advocate, having to make the case against unbridled altruism. But I do think there's a good case to be made, and not just by the devil.

I took some philosophy courses back in college, and as I thought about this question, the philosopher who kept coming up for me is Friedrich Nietzsche. Nietzsche thought that the Golden Rule has made us into a culture of wimps. He thought we'd been sold a bill of goods, mostly by Christianity, when we learned to divide people into "good," self-sacrificing people and "bad," self-serving people. He said we had lost the aristocratic virtues of ancient times—virtues like strength and nobility and self-affirmation. In fact, we have turned those values upside down, he said.

> **Nietzsche thought that the Golden Rule has made us into a culture of wimps.**

The weak don't want to be ruled by the strong, but there's no way they can take them on, so they label the strong "evil" and themselves "good"—out of resentment. In other words, good and evil have gotten defined by the losers. If you turn the other cheek, you're considered good in our culture, because we have been so influenced by Christianity. But Nietzsche says, if you turn the other cheek, it's probably because you don't think you're strong enough to hit back, and the only way you can get revenge is to label the strong guy bad. He says the "natural" values aren't good versus evil. The natural values are healthy versus sickly. The strong shouldn't feel guilty about wielding power. They should take their proper place at the head of the herd. And those who aren't strong shouldn't whine or moralize or feel superior because they turn the other cheek. They should either stand up for themselves or accept the authority of the strong.

Now, I know this sounds a lot like the Tea Party or Ayn Rand or something, but I don't want to take it that far. I feel society should give some extra help to people who are disadvantaged through no fault of their own, people who are born into poverty or who are old and frail or who are schizophrenic or whatever. And I know Nietzsche's philosophy was appropriated and misused by the Nazis. But I do think there's some truth in what he has to say.

I wouldn't relate it to the Tea Party so much as to— and I know this is going to sound silly—Oprah and Dr. Phil. I know, I know . . . ha, ha . . . but hear me out. I think it's important, maybe especially for us women, to not be doormats. We spent way too many years turning the other cheek. Nietzsche was right. That wasn't "good"; on the contrary, it was unhealthy! Unhealthy for us and unhealthy for our daughters.

So how does this apply to the person tied to the track? I'd say it would be unnatural, unhealthy for someone to flip the switch and divert the trolley to run over himself or herself, even if the trolley would otherwise kill five other people—and despite the fact that I would divert it to run over a total stranger. And, by the way, I wouldn't divert the trolley to run over my child or my husband or my mother or even my next-door neighbor, either. It wouldn't be natural. I have a strong tie to my relatives and friends, and it wouldn't be healthy—or true to myself—to sacrifice them for five strangers.

FRIEDRICH NIETZSCHE (1844–1900)

Nietzsche was born in the Prussian province of Saxony; his father was a Lutheran pastor. In 1864, he began studying theology and classical philology at the University of Bonn, but in the first semester he lost his faith and dropped the theology. He later famously declared the death of God and wrote scathing critiques of Christian ethics. He asserted that truly noble men are motivated not by pity for the weak, but by what he called the "will to power" and the affirmation of life. He thought that Christianity had inverted all the aristocratic values of the pre-Christian ancient world, replacing the natural assertiveness and pride of an Alexander the Great with what he considered to be the unhealthy humility of the Christian saints.

Nietzsche's notion of a life-affirming aristocracy of "supermen" was later twisted by the Nazis into the ideology of Arian supremacy, and as a result, Nietzsche's popularity took a downward turn after World War II. Nonetheless, Nietzsche had a profound influence on twentieth-century existentialists, as well as recent Continental thinkers, such as Michel Foucault and Jacques Derrida. Interestingly, Nietzsche's philosophy also influenced some religious thinkers, like the Jewish philosopher Martin Buber and the Christian theologian Paul Tillich.

All right, Stella. Good job. You've made a compelling case for self-affirmation. Marv, you have a two-minute rebuttal.

Well, I think Stella has made some good points, but I think her way of thinking is a slippery slope. It seems to me that it would be very easy to justify good old-fashioned selfishness by calling it natural or self-affirming. Instead of following the Golden Rule, I could give myself a golden parachute. Many of us have had bosses who lord it over their employees and probably feel they're just doing what comes naturally. And they are! Since when has what comes naturally become the standard, the thing we shoot for? You don't *have* to shoot for that. It's natural! If we're going to set a standard for ourselves, shouldn't it be something higher than following our natural disposition? Animals follow their natural dispositions. The thing that sets us apart from animals is that we aspire to a higher standard.

Stella?

Well, good point, Marv. But you have to draw the line somewhere on this altruism thing. I did a little "opposition research," as the politicians say, to prepare for tonight, so I read a bit about Professor Singer, too. According to the *New York Times,* he gives 20 percent of his income to famine relief agencies. That's twice as much as a tithe. It's very impressive. But why stop at 20 percent? I don't know how much Princeton professors earn, but I would imagine that he would have to give away more than 80 percent of his income if he were going to give away everything that he doesn't absolutely need for his own survival to help people somewhere in the world who lack necessities. I don't know what his justification is for stopping at 20 percent, but whatever it is, I'd like to claim it for my decision to not divert the trolley to run over me. I'm willing to be altruistic in some situations, but not at the cost of my life.

All right, excellent debate, Marv and Stella. Listeners, you've now heard the case for maximizing altruism and the case for setting limits on altruism. Now it's time for you to call in with your comments. We're especially interested in hearing from any of you who feel today's debate changed the way you think about the actual trolley trial.

Aaron Frobisher from Fargo, North Dakota, is on the line. Aaron?

Well, I think Marv is right, that the scenario in which he's both the switch-flipper and the guy on the track is very similar to the situation faced by Daphne Jones. But I draw the opposite conclusion. Marv says that if he is going to approve of Daphne Jones's action, he's obligated to expect the same behavior from himself.

But the analogy cuts the other way, too. If I'm *not* willing to divert the trolley to run over me, then I *shouldn't* approve of Daphne Jones's action. That's where the Golden Rule is useful. If I wouldn't do it to myself, then I shouldn't do it to Chet Farley. Frankly, I wouldn't do it to myself—I'm with Stella on that one. So, therefore, I shouldn't do it to Chet Farley, either. Or allow anyone else to do it. I guess that means I think Daphne Jones is guilty.

Hmm, very thought provoking. Interesting how we can take a principle like the Golden Rule and come to two opposite conclusions. But we've always known we have a very smart audience. Thank you, Aaron.

The phones are lighting up. Allison Boudreau from Tempe, Arizona, is on the line. What do you think, Allison?

Well, first of all, I'd like to disagree with the previous caller. No one is saying that Daphne Jones is *obligated* to pull the switch. I think it's *okay* for her to pull the switch—I don't think she should be found guilty. But I don't think it's her *duty* to pull the switch. She wouldn't be guilty of an ethical lapse if she had *not* pulled the switch. And I think it's okay if Marv wants to pull the switch and off himself, but I don't believe he's obligated to do that. So I don't think it logically follows that, just because the caller doesn't feel obligated to divert the trolley to hit himself, he should therefore condemn Daphne Jones for diverting it to hit Chet Farley. It's one of those situations where either acting or not acting is okay, but neither one is required of us.

All right. Thank you, Allison. What I hear you saying is that an action can be *permitted* without its being *required.* That might be a useful distinction for the jury to use in the Daphne Jones trial, eh?

Sarah Walters is calling from Dallas, Texas. Sarah?

I read somewhere about studies that show that men and women make ethical decisions differently. When women look at moral dilemmas, what tends to jump out for them is the relationships involved. What will happen to those relationships if I choose to take this tack rather than that one or that tack rather than this one? Men are more likely to see the same dilemma as an abstract issue: What is just? What is fair? Whose rights are violated?

As I was listening to Marv and Stella, I kept thinking that maybe the different conclusions they came to were because of the different ways they looked at the problem. Marv saw mostly the unfairness of allowing the trolley to run over Chet Farley if he wasn't willing to let it run over himself. (He didn't say what he'd do if the choice was letting the five be killed versus pulling the switch and allowing the trolley to run over a relative or a friend or a child. I bet he'd feel differently about that than he does about himself.) But, in any case, who the person on the track is and what my relationship to him or her is—and how that relationship may change depending on what I do—didn't jump out for Marv as the most striking thing.

What stood out for Stella, though, was that it makes a huge difference who the person on the siding is and what her relationship to that person is. She immediately thought of her child and her husband and her mother and her neighbor. And, yes, also herself.

I'm not sure they would have actually behaved all that differently. Marv even said he's not sure that in a real situation, he would actually sacrifice himself. But the point is that looking at the problem as a matter of abstract morality may come less immediately to mind for women than it does for men. Maybe men are more likely to see the question as sort of a math problem, where the people are sort of interchange-able parts, and women are more likely to see the question as a story—in which real people interact with real people.

What stood out for Stella was that it makes a huge difference who the person on the siding is and what her relationship to that person is.

Wow, another interesting and thoughtful perspective. It sounds like you may have read about Carol Gilligan's work in the 1980s, Sarah. Her book *In a Different Voice* studied adolescent girls and found that they saw ethical issues very differently from the way boys saw them.

Well, we've spent another fascinating hour with you, our listeners, as you debate and comment on the issues of the day. As always, the opinions of our participants have been well thought-out and articulately expressed.

We hope you'll listen in next week, when our topic will be: Should the government regulate risky personal behavior? We'll look at regulations on everything from seat belts to sugary beverages. Until then, this is Jeff Salaby, on behalf of *NPR Debates,* saying, "Mind your pros and cons!"

THE FACULTY'S COLLOQUY

/////////////////////////

Faculty Lounge

SCHOOL OF ADVANCED STUDY
UNIVERSITY OF LONDON
Monday, April 22, 2013

In attendance: **Nigel Straithwaite, Professor of British** History; Liz Wilkinson, Professor of Applied Mathematics; Theodore Payne, Senior Lecturer in Engineering; Alistair Fox, Professor of Philosophy; and Abiodun Nzeogwu, Lecturer in Political Science.

NIGEL: Have any of you been following this court case in the States? The man who got run over by the tram?

LIZ: Yes. Fascinating. The defendant saved five lives by diverting the tram, but they want to put her away because she sacrificed one man's life. It wouldn't surprise me if the five people she saved were all women, and the District Attorney thought their lives weren't worth the life of one man.

TED: Do you have a problem with that, Liz?

LIZ: It would depend on how attractive the man was, Ted.

NIGEL: It reminded me of a decision that Churchill made during the war. I have the students in my history tutorial reading about the Battle of Britain. I had forgotten that, in the beginning, the Nazis' VI rockets were actually falling rather short of their target, landing in South East London, about two miles south of the center of the city. Churchill's top brass came up with a plan to use a double agent to deceive the Germans into thinking that the doodlebugs were actually falling in North West London. The idea was to get them to adjust their aim so that the rockets fell even farther to the southeast, where they would kill fewer people. The sticky wicket, of course, was that the people who would now be hit were different people, people who were in no danger before. The top brass agonized about the morality of the plan, and Herbert Morrison, the minister for home security, was adamantly opposed to it. In the end, Winnie overruled him, and I say, thank God! As it was, the doodlebugs killed 6,000 people. God only knows how many more people they would have killed if Churchill had given in.

Liz: That does sound a lot like the decision this Daphne Jones made: save five, lose one. She didn't really intend to kill the poor bloke on the siding, any more than the prime minister meant to kill the people of South East London. She didn't *use* his death to stop the tram, like that daft American a few years back who threw a man in front of a runaway tram to save people on the track.

Nigel: My point exactly.

Liz: By the way, does it strike anyone else that the Americans have a bit of a runaway tram problem? I've never heard of a tram in the U.K. running amok.

Ted: That's the question my engineering students are most interested in. Statistically, the U.S. has more fatal tram accidents than Zimbabwe. The kids in my class want to go for the fix.

In our discussion, one of my students brought up an interesting idea. It's not a solution by any means, but it does shed some light on the morality of the issue. She wondered how we'd think about what Daphne Jones did if, instead of there being a straight siding, the track had looped around and rejoined the main track, and the five people were even farther down the main track.

Nigel: Huh?

Ted: Here, I'll draw it for you.

My student pointed out that in this scenario the body of the man on the siding—assuming the bloke weighed at least 127 kilos—would have stopped the tram and prevented it from hitting the five people. She said she still thought Daphne should have pulled the switch, even though in this case she would have *intended* to kill the man . . . Farley, his name was Farley. In the actual court case, Daphne diverted the tram onto a straight siding that did not rejoin the main track, so she might conceivably have hoped Farley would somehow get out of the way in time, although it was clear that that was impossible. In any case, the tram's hitting the man was just an unintended consequence of saving the five people. In the loop story, she has to hope the man *doesn't* get out of the way. She *needs* the tram to hit him. She *does* use his death to save the five others. Still, my student said, she'd pull the switch.

LIZ: What did you say to the student?

TED: I told her she got a First in engineering, but failed ethics.

Actually, I asked her if she would have pushed the fat guy off the bridge. She said no. I asked her why, and she said in the loop story, there's already a real danger. The tram is going to hit and kill *someone.* If I pull the switch, I'm just diverting that danger from five people to one, just like Daphne pulling the switch. But the guy who pushed the fat man off the bridge didn't just divert the danger of the tram's hitting someone. He *created* a brand-*new* danger—the danger of being a fat guy on that bridge.

NIGEL: Hmm. That seems pretty abstract to me. The guy's dead either way. What difference does it make whether we kill him by throwing him in front of the tram or by sending the tram to run over him?

TED: Well, that's the question, isn't it? But you could also ask the same question about Daphne's case versus throwing the man off the bridge. If the man ends up dead either way, what difference does it make how he got there? And yet, I do think it makes a big difference whether you throw the switch or throw the man. My student was just drawing the line at a different place, saying it wasn't Daphne's intention that was important, but rather whether she merely diverted a threat or created a new one.

LIZ: Hmm. I'm changing my position. I think I partially agree with your student, but I would draw the line in yet a different way. I think she's correct that Daphne's case and the loop case are both different from throwing the big bloke off the bridge. And, like her, I think switching the tram to a straight siding or to a looped siding are both morally permissible, while throwing the guy off the bridge is morally wrong. But I don't think it has anything to do with diverting threats versus creating them. I think what made it wrong for the man to push the big bloke off the bridge is that it involved personal force. Think about it. If you didn't have to *push* the guy—like, say, he was standing on a trap door, and all you had to do is push a button and the trap door would open and he'd fall on the track—wouldn't you do it? I think I would.

ALISTAIR: Jesus, I wouldn't! You're all trying to dream up some subtle factor that makes it okay to pull a switch but not okay to push a man off the bridge. Nigel, you think it has to do with Daphne's lack of intent to kill Farley and her not using his death as a means to save the five. Ted, your student thinks it has to do with diverting a danger that already exists versus creating a new one. Liz, you think it's about using personal force. You're all making this way too complicated.

LIZ: How so?

ALISTAIR: Both Daphne's innocence and the guilt of
the guy who pushed the fat fellow to his death simply
stem from old Jerry Bentham's principle of the greatest
happiness for the greatest number. Period. The D.A.
in the case was wrong. Bentham's utilitarian principle
doesn't dictate that it's permissible to harvest a healthy
man's vital organs or push the man in front of the tram.
How come? It's because the guy who pushed the man
didn't *really* bring about the greatest happiness for the
greatest number.

LIZ: You're losing me.

ALISTAIR: You can't just look at his act in a vacuum.
He violated a *rule* that must be followed *in order to bring
about* the greatest happiness for the greatest number.
The rule is: "Avoid scaring the bejeezus out of the whole
population." Society would be chaotic and scary as hell
if people generally followed the lead of the guy who
pushed the fat man, killing someone every time it would
save a greater number, like those kidney police we heard

about in the trial. But many people *do* behave as Daphne did, and society actually rewards them, because we don't feel our personal security is threatened. Think of how we praise airline pilots who choose to crash-land their plane away from major population centers so that fewer people on the ground will be killed. Granted, the pilot doesn't have the choice of doing nothing, as Daphne did, but that factor doesn't seem to matter to the public. Daphne's action didn't scare most people until the prosecutor decided to try to scare them. And throwing the man off the bridge did scare people.

Daphne's action didn't scare most people until the prosecutor decided to try to scare them.

If you look merely at the lives of five versus the life of one, you might think Bentham would approve of throwing the man in front of the tram or harvesting the organs of a healthy person. That's what caused the D.A. to go into his anti-Bentham rant. But Bentham would have looked at the broader picture and seen that the pain of a frightened population trumps the pleasure of the five whose lives were saved.

ABIODUN: If I may add a little Third World perspective here, I've been listening to all of you, and you all seem to want to let Daphne Jones off the hook. I'm not so sure that's the answer. She really was playing God. And if we're going to play God, we'd better be damned sure we're as unbiased as God allegedly is. Who *was* this guy on the siding, anyway? I have to wonder if Americans would feel differently about the case if the guy on the siding were a yacht-owning billionaire named Channing Ellsworth III than if he were an inner-city janitor named Latrell Payton. Would a majority of Americans be more likely to spare a rich white guy than a poor member of an ethnic or racial minority? Truth to tell, I'm not sure I wouldn't be more likely to spare Latrell. I know I shouldn't, but I can't say for sure what I *would* do.

NIGEL: Well, *that* was a conversation stopper, Abiodun.

ABIODUN: I know. I did it because I have to get to my class now, and I didn't want to miss any of the discussion!

THE JUDGE'S CHARGE

///////////////////////////////

Instructions to the Jury

Judge Harlan Trueworthy

COURT OF PUBLIC OPINION
Monday, April 22, 2013

Ladies and gentlemen of the jury, you have now listened to the evidence from both the prosecution and the defense in the case of *The People v. Daphne Jones.* The moment of truth has arrived, and it is now time for you to deliberate and reach a verdict. You must find Ms. Jones either guilty or not guilty of voluntary manslaughter in the death of Chester "Chet" Farley.

Much of the argument on both sides has been over the strength or weakness of various analogies. While you are free to decide this case by any method you choose, you may wish to test these analogies and determine whether they do the work they are apparently being asked to do. Is pulling the switch really essentially the same ethically as throwing someone in the path of the trolley or removing someone's vital organs?

Please notice, however, that deciding whether these analogies "work" is not the end of the matter. If you were to decide, for example, that throwing the switch *is* essentially the same as throwing someone off a bridge, do you conclude from that that both perpetrators are guilty or that both are innocent? Similarly, if you conclude that throwing the switch is *not* ethically the same as throwing someone in the path of the trolley, that conclusion alone will not tell you whether either perpetrator is guilty or innocent.

> **Is pulling the switch really the same ethically as throwing someone in the path of the trolley?**

So you have a very complex decision to make. In the Court of Public Opinion you may decide this case, if you wish, by consulting tarot cards or throwing darts at a board. I do not mean to trivialize your options, but rather to make a point. While most of you will not consult the tarot, there will be many of you who might wish to say, "My opinion just feels right, and nothing can convince me otherwise." And perhaps trusting our feelings of right and wrong *is* in the end the way we must make ethical decisions. The court does not have an opinion on this matter. But I *would* caution you against settling too comfortably for the second part of that statement: "and nothing can convince me otherwise." We all know that what felt right last night may very well feel wrong this morning. So I would urge you at the very least to take seriously the various arguments put forth in the case and try, to the extent possible, to back up your moral intuitions with reasons.

And with that, I turn the case over to you for deliberation.

THE JURY'S DECISION

////////////////////

Jury Room 4

COURT OF PUBLIC OPINION
Monday, April 22, 2013

Good morning, everyone. I'm Serena Hernandez, your foreman . . . or forewoman . . . or foreperson, I suppose. We've compiled the opinions of all the associate jurors out there in the public arena, and you've all presumably had time to review them. So let's jump right in. Does anyone want to share how they see this case right now? This doesn't mean that you can't change your mind after you hear what everyone else has to say. It's just that we have to start somewhere. So . . . anyone? Please introduce yourselves when you speak.

Okay, I'll start. I'm Maureen, and I'm a health-policy analyst in the U.S. Department of Health and Human Services. Every time we decide to cover some health-care interventions and not cover others, we are making decisions that may have undesirable consequences for some people. Neither side in the debate about the Affordable Care Act (or Obamacare, if you will) has been totally candid about this.

There are, of course, no "death panels" in the act, but there *is* an advisory board that will make policy recommendations to Congress about the best medical practices and how to incentivize them. Suppose they recommend that a certain treatment is not the best practice because it spends billions of Medicare dollars to provide a few days of extra life to a few people. The panel's justification is that it would be far more cost-effective to spend that money on preventive services for thousands of people. If Congress adopts their recommendation, they will, in effect, have chosen a good path with an undesirable consequence.

And as long as the good clearly outweighs the bad, that's okay! That's what policy decisions do—allocate limited resources to do the most good. If there were an infinite amount of money available, we could do everything patients and families want done. Unfortunately, that isn't reality. We never have infinite resources.

Daphne Jones did not have infinite options, either. If she were Wonder Woman, she could have found a solution that kept all lives intact. She could have lifted the trolley or moved the track or any one of a hundred options that the comic book writers of our youth were so good at dreaming up. But Ms. Jones had only two options, and she chose the one that would do the most good—even though it had a very undesirable consequence for Mr. Farley. We should find her not guilty.

Thank you, Maureen. Yes, the gentleman next to Maureen.

Hello, everybody. I'm Steve, and I'm a captain in the U.S. Army. When I was at West Point, they gave us a lot of training on the difference between deliberately killing civilians and accidentally causing the death of civilians when we attack a military target. Al-Qaeda deliberately attacks civilians, and as a result, we rightly brand them terrorists. When they destroyed the World Trade Center, it was not because it was a legitimate military target. They destroyed it precisely because it would kill a large number of innocent civilians.

When we send our drones from Afghanistan across the Pakistan border to kill enemy personnel, sometimes we kill innocent civilians, but we don't intend to do that. It happens as an unwanted consequence of our doing something that's right and proper, defending our nation from our enemies. We can pretty much foresee sometimes that "collateral damage" (that's what the army calls the unintended death of civilians) is likely to happen, but we don't *want* it to happen.

Here's the test, I think. If the drone attack did *not* kill any civilians, we would be pleased. In fact, if there were any way that we could get the civilians out of there before the attack, or maybe choose a time of day when we knew the civilians would not be there, we would do that. When Al-Qaeda attacked the World Trade Center, on the other hand, they deliberately chose a day and a time when they could kill as many civilians as possible. So let's say, unbeknownst to Al-Qaeda, it was Labor Day here, and there were very few people in the Twin Towers at the time of the attack. Bin Laden would have been bitterly disappointed.

If Ms. Jones could have saved the five people without killing Mr. Farley, I believe she would have done so. We should therefore find her not guilty. Thank you.

Thank you, Steve. Okay, let's hear from the man across the table from me.

Hello. I'm Darren, and I teach philosophy at the state university. You could say I'm a professional utilitarian. I think Daphne Jones is not guilty. No surprise there. But here's the thing: I also think Frank Tremaine, the man who threw the guy off the bridge, is not guilty. Steve here is looking for a way to differentiate the case of Frank Tremaine from the case of Daphne Jones. He feels he needs a reason to find Frank guilty and Daphne not guilty. But, in fact, they both chose the course that brought about the greatest happiness for the greatest number of people.

Why do we find Frank's act so repellent? It's because our so-called intuition makes us squeamish about throwing someone off a bridge into the path of an oncoming trolley, specifically in order to kill him and thereby save five others. I must admit it makes me squeamish, too. But there are a lot of things that make us squeamish—throwing ourselves on a hand grenade to save our platoon, for example—but they're still the right thing to do. Of course, some of us are more squeamish about harming someone else for the common good than harming our-selves, but the common good is, by definition, the course that brings about the *most* good. So we shouldn't allow our emotions to get in the way of our reason. Every phi-losopher since Socrates has warned us that that is the road to perdition.

Even in military history, Steve, there have been times when deliberately killing civilians was judged to be the right course on strictly utilitarian grounds. I would argue that the nuclear bombing of the citizens of Hiroshima and Nagasaki was justified, because it brought the war to an end, and the world as a whole was a better place.

Provocative point, Darren. I suppose that was the official justification at the time, but a lot of people would be offended by the idea today. Fortunately, that's not the question before us. So, anyone else? The gentleman sit-ting next to Darren.

Yes, I'm Siegfried and I'm a psychiatrist. This chat-ter about throwing people off bridges—that's crazy talk, Darren. You know this, I hope, yes?

After the Frank Tremaine case was decided, a couple of my colleagues did a study of the people who thought Mr. Tremaine had behaved correctly in choosing the utilitarian option of pushing the man off the bridge to save the five others. Their hypothesis was that the people who decided that Mr. Tremaine did the right thing would generally turn out to be (a) more psychopathic, (b) more Machiavellian, and (c) more nihilistic, more likely to think that life is meaningless.

They devised some tests to measure whether a person is any of those things and gave the tests to a number of people who thought Mr. Tremaine was guilty and to a like number of those who thought he was innocent. It turned out that there was a strong link between approving of Mr. Tremaine's pushing the man off the bridge and the likelihood of being all three: psychopathic, Machiavellian, and nihilistic. Very interesting, eh?

There was a strong link between approving of pushing the man off the bridge and the likelihood of being psychopathic, Machiavellian, and nihilistic.

Hmm. Yes, Siegfried, very interesting. Although I'm not sure what that says about *Daphne's* guilt or innocence. Anyone else?

Hi. Leland here. I'm a novelist. I think it's interesting that we are all trying to sort out who it's okay to kill or allow to die, without any information at all about who these people are. What novelists do is try to imagine the particulars in the situation. Maybe, for all we know, the five people somehow enticed Chet Farley to the siding, knowing that Daphne would likely throw the switch and kill him—the perfect crime. Okay, that's pretty far out. But if anyone's thinking it's a case of the greatest happiness for the greatest number, we also need a lot more information to make that assessment. Maybe it will be revealed that one of the five people Daphne saved is a child molester or sexual predator. Or maybe one of them will go on to discover a cure for cancer—that's good, right?—but, in a cruel twist, a woman she cures will give birth to a baby who will grow up to be a serial killer.

These plots are all pulp fiction, I know, but my point is that we simply don't know enough about what we're doing

NICCOLÒ MACHIAVELLI (1469–1527)

Like the words *Platonic* and *Socratic*, *Machiavellian* is an instance of a philosopher's name having crossed over into common parlance: in today's jargon, a meme.

Machiavelli was born in Florence at the height of the Italian Renaissance, as the theological values of the medieval world were rapidly giving way to new humanist ways of thinking, and the secular state was flourishing, largely untethered from its old alliances with the Church. Machiavelli, in his position as secretary to the government of the Republic of Florence, based his political advice not on classical or medieval ideals of virtue but on the realities of gaining and maintaining secular power. He may or may not have been more ruthless in that pursuit than other politicians of his—or our—day, but he was certainly more candid about it. For example, he urged that the prince ought to "enter into evil when necessitated."

Delving deeper into the study that Siegfried, the psychiatrist, mentions, we learn that people were labeled "Machiavellian" if they agreed with the statement "The best way to handle people is to tell them what they want to hear." Machiavelli may or may not have been Machiavellian by that standard, depending on whether he thought it would enhance the power of the prince—and whether he thought the prince could get away with it.

to make neat, ethical decisions. We may think we're deciding the case on the basis of the consequences, but who among us ever knows what the consequences will be? That's the biggest reason we shouldn't play God! And also the biggest reason we shouldn't treat the case as a math problem, for God's sake. "Five is greater than one" doesn't do it. Maybe in this instance the one—Mr. Farley—was way greater than the five. Daphne Jones is guilty of playing God. She should have done nothing and just let fate take its course.

Well, Leland, by your reasoning, wouldn't doctors be reluctant to save the life of *anybody* for fear they might turn out to be a serial killer?

Yeah, maybe. Let me try a somewhat different tack. It's my belief that, regardless of what we say our reasons are, most of us are going to judge this case by how it strikes us emotionally. And our emotional response is going to be pretty much determined by the kind of story we each tell ourselves about this case. Do we identify Mr. Farley, for example, with our father? Does that predispose us to feel positively about him and therefore outraged at his arbitrary death? Or, if our dad was a son-of-a-bitch, do we feel negatively about him and wonder what mischief he was up to when he was walking on that track? We can try to put all of these reactions out of our minds, but the fact remains that how we judge Ms. Jones is by and large dependent on whether we think *we* would have pulled the switch. And, if we're honest, we have to admit that whether we would have done it probably depends heavily on our picture of who the person on the siding was. The only safe rule is "Don't play God."

Is anyone else leaning toward finding Daphne Jones guilty?

Yes, I am. Hi, everyone. I'm Marguerite, and I'm an attorney for Human Rights Watch. Steve, you seemed to be saying that there's a big difference between "collateral damage" (such as Chet Farley, I guess) and the deliberate killing of an innocent person, like the man on the bridge. Darren says he doesn't see much difference between throwing the switch and pushing the man, so he thinks both Daphne Jones and Frank Tremaine are not guilty.

I agree with Darren insofar as I don't see much difference, either, but I reach the opposite conclusion: I think both Daphne and Frank are guilty. Both of them violated the rights of the person they killed, or, if you prefer, "allowed to die." We have a *duty* to not throw someone in the path of a trolley or harvest their organs, no matter how good the consequences may be, just as we at Human Rights Watch believe we have a duty to not engage in torture, no matter what information we might uncover. Likewise, we have a duty to not divert a trolley to run over a person, no matter how good the consequences. It matters little to Chet Farley's loved ones whether the perpetrator actively killed him or only put in motion a course that allowed him to die. To rely on that distinction would be like saying, "We don't torture; we merely turn prisoners over to another country where we will allow them to be tortured." And, yes, I know that was precisely the position of our government at one time, but that tells us only that our government in that instance acted immorally.

Thank you, Marguerite. The woman with the lovely blue scarf?

Hi, I'm Nancy, and I'm an artist, a painter actually. After each of you has spoken, I've found myself agreeing with you. Your arguments are all very persuasive—until I hear the next one. But, in the end, I think Daphne Jones is not guilty and Frank Tremaine is guilty, and I can't say exactly why. . . . I just feel it in my bones. I guess I'd call it "intuition." I just *know* that what Frank Tremaine did in throwing that man off the bridge is wrong, plainly and simply wrong. And what Daphne did doesn't feel the same to me at all. I don't think it's because I have particular emotional connections to people in the case, as Leland was saying. My decision doesn't seem emotional to me; it seems intuitive. That's all I have to say. Sorry if that doesn't sound very cogent, but that's the bottom line for me. They just feel different, and I don't have a clue why they do. They just do!

Thank you. Anyone else? No? Then are we ready to vote? Okay. Those who think we should find Daphne Jones guilty of voluntary manslaughter? Okay. Those in favor of finding Daphne Jones not guilty of voluntary manslaughter? All right, then. The jury has spoken.

[For the verdict, see next page.]

Now, really, you didn't seriously think there'd be an answer here, did you?

EPILOGUE

////////////////////////////

Where Have We Landed?

Trolleyology is entertaining, but where does it leave us? After following poor Daphne Jones through all the vicissitudes of her trial, are we any wiser than we were when we set out?

Some may believe, like Nancy the juror, that in the end we all make our moral decisions by gut feel, and therefore all the analysis in the world is really just our rationalizing of our moral intuitions. In this view, there would seem to be little value—other than perhaps entertainment—in thinking about the basis of the moral distinctions we draw, such as the difference most feel between throwing a switch and throwing a man. We may claim to "know" in some visceral way that the one is permissible and the other is not, and we may therefore feel that any deliberation or articulation is merely rationalization. Much trolleyology in the philosophical literature does, in fact, follow that pattern: what Peter Singer calls the "search for differences between the cases that justify our initial intuitive responses." If moral reasoning comes down to rationalization, one might well ask, "Why bother?" Perhaps Socrates just had it wrong when he said that the unexamined life is not worth leading.

A Notre Dame University sociologist, Christian Smith, recently caused a stir with the publication of his study of "emerging adults" (eighteen- to twenty-three-year-olds) and how they think about morality—if in fact they think about it at all. Smith expresses concern that a large percentage of the young adults he interviewed did not think in a rigorous or coherent way about moral issues. Many (30 percent) expressed a strong moral relativism that allowed them to say, for example, that while they personally do not steal or cheat, they would not judge one of their friends who did. "It's all up to what the individual thinks," many said. Smith's point is not so much that he thinks such a moral stance is wrong (although one would guess that he does), but rather that he sees it as an inability to *think coherently* about moral issues. When asked, for example, whether slavery was morally right before it was banned, some responded that they were not able to judge the way people in another time thought or behaved. Smith thinks this point of view is neither carefully thought out nor logically coherent.

Smith sees this inability to articulate moral views as the downside of an otherwise admirable trend in our public education: the positive value we have increasingly placed on tolerance of other points of view and the understanding of other cultures and social groups. When tolerance is stretched to the point of relativizing all other values, Smith sees a lack of rigorous moral reasoning. Such shallow thinking, he says, is "unable to result in good moral decision making and a morally coherent life. And that is a form of impoverishment."

Yet Smith and his colleagues refuse to say that the actual behavior of today's young people is any worse than that of their more morally articulate predecessors. Most slave owners, after all, probably had "principled" opinions about the justification of slavery. We know that some of them, for example, appealed to scripture. So we come back to the question of why moral philosophy matters. What difference, if any, does moral reasoning make?

First, let's sort out one overlapping issue. Some philosophers think that the trolley problem is so far removed from ordinary human experience and real ethical dilemmas that it is trivial. One unnamed philosopher, approached on the subject by a British journalist, said, "I'm sorry, I just don't do trolleys." Perhaps in that respect, the trolley problem is similar to a scenario that we are all familiar with from the justification of the use of torture on known or suspected terrorists: the so-called ticking time bomb. After 9/11, many politicians justified torturing detainees by creating a scenario in which many lives hang in the balance while a terrorist refuses to give up the one key piece of information that will save them. As it happens, that scenario bears almost no resemblance to what is at issue in 99 percent of actual interrogations. Yet it became the template for nearly all public discussion of torture. So one conclusion we might draw is that extreme scenarios like runaway trolleys and ticking time bombs are without value in clarifying our ethical decisions.

But another conclusion we might draw is that, if we all simply relied on our intuition about terrorism and ticking time bombs, we would come to a very different moral judgment about torture than we would if we *analyzed* the actual use of torture and drew a careful distinction between it and the ticking time bomb scenario.

Perhaps applying our moral reasoning to the differences between the trolley problem and a particular real-life decision may also turn out to be helpful. Moreover, while it could hardly be argued that the trolley problem represents an ethical decision we are likely to be called upon to make in real life, learning to draw the distinction between individual rights and the happiness of the greatest number may, in fact, become a factor in a real ethical decision. It certainly did for the framers of the U.S. Constitution. And, more recently, we as voters in presidential and congressional elections have been asked to decide between the supposed property *rights* of people who choose not to buy health insurance and the supposed greater *utility* of using those mandated premiums to fund health insurance for people with preexisting conditions.

Do we sometimes use moral reasoning to find a rationalization for our intuitions? Of course. But does rigorous moral reasoning sometimes change our intuitions about the rightness or wrongness of an action? Also yes. The abolition of slavery came about in part because people with one intuition outthought people with the opposite intuition. And a change in our intuitions about marriage is happening before our eyes, as moral arguments, based on equality and fairness, are heard in legislatures and judges' chambers, as well as around the dinner table.

Which is all to say, with apologies to Yogi Berra: When your trolley comes to a fork in the track, take it.

And be able to say why you did.

SOURCE NOTES

///////////////////////////////

PROLOGUE: THE PROBLEMATIC TROLLEY

Philippa Foot's original version of the trolley problem appeared in an article called "The Problem of Abortion and the Doctrine of the Double Effect," in the British journal *Oxford Review*, No. 5 (1967).

Judith Jarvis Thomson's variation of the bystander and the switch appeared in "The Trolley Problem," *Yale Law Journal* (1985), as did the variation of the large man on the bridge.

Kwame Appiah's comparison of trolley problem commentary to the Talmud appeared in his book *Experiments in Ethics* (Harvard University Press, 2008).

The Moral Sense Test developed by Harvard psychologists in 2003 can be found online at: moral.wjh.harvard.edu.

The PBS video of Michael Sandel's lectures for his Harvard College course on justice can be found at: justiceharvard.org. He talks about the trolley problem in episode 01.

THE PROSECUTOR'S THRUST

Jeremy Bentham outlines his utilitarian philosophy in *An Introduction to the Principles of Morals and Legislation* (Nabu Press, 2010).

The scenario of the trauma surgeon appears in Judith Jarvis Thomson's 1985 *Yale Law Journal* article. Related scenarios can be found in Philippa Foot's 1967 *Oxford Review* piece.

A more or less accessible version (perhaps more "less" than "more") of Kant's position on rights can be found in his *Groundwork of the Metaphysics of Morals* (Cambridge University Press, 1999).

THE DEFENSE ATTORNEY'S PARRY

The opinions of the subjects taking the Moral Sense Test online are discussed by Marc Hauser et al. in a lengthy article entitled "A Dissociation Between Moral Judgments and Justifications," in the journal *Mind and Language* 22, no. 1 (February 2007).

THE PROFESSOR'S ANALYSIS

David Hume's *Dialogues Concerning Natural Religion* is available in a 2007 edition from Neeland Media.

THE PSYCHOLOGIST'S OPINION

A summary of the results of functional MRI studies of moral decision-making can be found in Joshua Greene's unpublished doctoral dissertation, *The Terrible, Horrible, No Good, Very Bad Truth About Morality, and What to Do About It* (Princeton University, 2002). Greene is a psychologist, neuroscientist, and philosopher.

A good discussion of the link between our aversion to killing and the experience of our distant ancestors can be found in Peter Singer's article "Ethics and Intuitions," in the *Journal of Ethics* 9 (2005).

G. E. Moore sets out the naturalistic fallacy in *Principia Ethica* (Cambridge University Press, 1903).

THE BISHOP'S BRIEF

St. Thomas's explication of the Principle of Double Effect is found in his *Summa Theologiae* IIa–IIae, Question 64, Article 7, published in English by Coyote Canyon Press (2010).

The Catholic Church's modern version of the Principle of Double Effect can be found in *The New Catholic Encyclopedia* (Gale, 2002).

The explanation of the Church's position on the application of the Principle of Double Effect to a woman with cancer of the uterus appears in Arne Hallam's online editorial introduction to Philippa Foot's article, "The Problem of Abortion and the Doctrine of the Double Effect." It can be accessed at: www2.econ.iastate.edu/classes/econ362/hallam/readings/footdoubleeffect.pdf.

The application of the Principle of Double Effect to the administration of morphine is from the online article by Richard M. Doerflinger and Carlos F. Gomez, M.D., Ph.D., "Killing the Pain, Not the Patient: Palliative Care vs. Assisted Suicide," published online by the U.S. Conference of Catholic Bishops at: usccb.org/issues-and-action/human-life-and-dignity/assisted-suicide/killing-the-pain.cfm.

THE ALTRUIST'S DILEMMA

I owe the scenario of the decider tied to the track to a comment by "Duoae" at Chris Bateman's 2007 "Only a Game" blog: onlyagame.typepad.com/only_a_game/2007/06/the-trolley-pro.html.

Peter Singer's scenarios are found in two *New York Times* articles: "The Life You Can Save" (March 10, 2009) and "The Singer Solution to World Poverty" (September 5, 1999). The 1999 article also poses the question of why Professor Singer draws the line for philanthropy at 20 percent of his income.

There is a recent English translation of Nietzsche's *Beyond Good and Evil* published by Costa Books (2012).

I owe the question of whether one who is unwilling to sacrifice herself for five should be entitled to sacrifice another for five to Judith Jarvis Thomson's article "Turning the Trolley," in *Philosophy and Public Affairs* 36, no. 4 (2008). In the 1985 *Yale Law Journal* article "The Trolley Problem," she makes the helpful distinction between permissible and obligatory actions.

The discussion of the different ways men and women tend to approach moral dilemmas relies heavily on my understanding of Carol Gilligan's landmark book, *In a Different Voice* (Harvard University Press, 1982).

THE FACULTY'S COLLOQUY

The true story of the deception of the Nazis in the Battle of Britain is told by Ben Macintyre in *Agent Zigzag: A True Story of Nazi Espionage, Love, and Betrayal* (Crown, 2007).

The train track loop scenario was invented by Judith Jarvis Thomson and explained in her 1985 article "The Trolley Problem," in the *Yale Law Journal*.

The experiment in which the trap door scenario is posed to experimental subjects is described by Joshua Greene at: edge.org/conversation/a-new-science-of-morality-part-2.

For a discussion of "rule utilitarianism," see R. B. Brandt, *Ethical Theory* (Prentice Hall, 1959).

The scenario involving Latrell Payton and Channing Ellsworth III is adapted from an experiment conducted by Eric Luis Uhlmann, David A. Pizarro, David Tannenbaum, and Peter H. Ditto and reported in the October 2009 edition of the journal *Judgment and Decision Making*. In the actual experiment, the large man on the bridge scenario was used. Interestingly, conservatives were apparently unbiased, while liberals were more likely to sacrifice the stereotypical blueblood than the stereotypical African American.

SOURCE NOTES

THE JURY'S DECISION

The teaching of the Principle of Double Effect at the
U.S. Military Academy at West Point is documented in
an interesting article about the trolley problem by David
Edmonds in the October 7, 2010, edition of the British
periodical *Prospect Magazine*. The article can be found online
at: prospectmagazine.co.uk/magazine/ethics-trolley-problem/.

Mr. Edmonds's article also contains an interesting
discussion of the allocation of scarce resources, which is
reflected in the juror's analysis of health policy.

The psychiatrist's conclusion about the correlation between
certain negative personality traits and the person's willingness
to push the heavyset man off the bridge is based on a study
done by Daniel Bartels and David Pizarro and reported in
the journal *Cognition* (2011). The report was titled "The
Mismeasure of Morals: Antisocial Personality Traits Predict
Utilitarian Responses to Moral Dilemmas" and can be found
online at: columbia.edu/~dmb2199/papers/
Bartels-Pizarro-2011-Cognition.pdf.

The novelist's perfect-crime fantasy was suggested by a
similar scenario in Judith Jarvis Thomson's 1985 *Yale Law
Journal* article.

Some of the novelist's more rococo scenarios were inspired by an online parody (1988) of the trolley literature by Michael F. Patton Jr. See "Tissues in the Profession: Can Bad Men Make Good Brains Do Bad Things?" at: mindspring.com/~mfpatton/Tissues.htm.

EPILOGUE: WHERE HAVE WE LANDED?

Christian Smith's study of the moral reasoning of young adults is titled *Lost in Transition: The Dark Side of Emerging Adulthood* (Oxford University Press, 2011).